BEACHED IN CALABRIA

IAN ROSS

Arcadia Books Ltd
139 Highlever Road
London W10 6PH

www.arcadiabooks.co.uk

First published in the United Kingdom 2019
Copyright © Ian Ross 2019
Cover illustrations © Honey Ross 2019

A catalogue record for this book is available from the British Library.

ISBN 978-1-911350-62-0

Typeset in Garamond by MacGuru Ltd
Printed and bound by TJ International, Padstow PL28 8RW

ARCADIA BOOKS DISTRIBUTORS ARE AS FOLLOWS:

in the UK and elsewhere in Europe:
BookSource
50 Cambuslang Road
Cambuslang
Glasgow G32 8NB

in Australia/New Zealand:
NewSouth Books
University of New South Wales
Sydney NSW 2052

BEACHED IN CALABRIA

ALSO BY IAN ROSS

Rocking the Boat
Beverly Hills Butler

IAN ROSS was born in Chelsea in 1943. Aged sixteen he went to Los Angeles, saw an automatic car wash and opened one in Richmond, Britain's first. In 1963, he co-founded Pirate Station Radio Caroline, briefly co-managed The Animals, and met his future wife Bunty Lampson. He moved his family to Los Angeles in 1979 and opened Flipper's Roller Boogie Palace in Hollywood. The place caused a sensation and was closed by the authorities after three years whereupon Ian became a butler in Beverly Hills. In 1988 he returned to England and wrote two books about his adventures, *Rocking the Boat* and *Beverly Hills Butler*, both published by Heinemann.

To Bunty
Wife, love of my life

and

To Dottore Pino Toscano, Pasquale Pangallo,
Giovanni 'Gianni' Nocera and their families, who made
this story possible, with gratitude and affection

Contents

Apologia Italiana   ix

1. Sempre Problemi   1
2. Et in Calabria Ego   17
3. The Pinos   29
4. How to Buy a House   37
5. Viaggio con il Diavolo   51
6. How to Build a House   59
7. The Family System   71
8. Piano Piano   79
9. Costa Nostra   89
10. The Sea Has Eyes   105
11. Mad Dogs and Englishmen   109
12. Going Fast Slowly   119
13. The Devil in the Garden   129
14. My Family and Other   137
15. La Musica!   147
16. Celebrity Kidnapping   157
17. The Green Vote   165
18. Vigile!   177
19. How to Buy a Pig   187
20. The Immense Fence   195
21. Post Script   203
     Epilogue   209

Acknowledgements   213

Contents

Apologia Italiana

In this book I have attempted to describe conversations with my Calabrese friends and others as best I can in words as spoken and understood by me. This does not mean, and I apologise for it, that the language, grammar, spelling, etc. are accurate or true of conversational, or written, Italian, Calabrese, dialetto, etc.

One of the wonders of our little Altro Mondo is that little or no English is spoken, and this, as well as being in a unique Old Italy time warp, is one of the most refreshing aspects of stopping the world and getting off at the Jasmine Coast. No English Voices means you're cut off from most of the bad news in the world, and most of what you do hear you can't understand.

I had to cobble together a means of communication with my friends Pasquale, Pino and Gianni and co. and at least *we* understand it. I thought it best and simplest to reproduce it for you 'warts and all' rather than attempt to correct it, which would, in my view, take away rather than add to both the sense and any entertainment value you might hopefully derive from this book.

So ciao, read on, enjoy.

Ian Ross

Sempre Problemi

I'm sitting under an olive tree called Stumpy, on the tiled barakka terrace we built facing directly onto our beach, drinking a cup of caffè Inglese, my first of the day, and gazing out over our sandy little smile of a bay, our small slice of blue Mediterranean heaven.

The morning sun has risen over the lighthouse as it always does – there's been one there for 3,000 years, and there are 326 days of sunshine a year here on the Jasmine Coast. At seven a.m. it is warm on my face, and bright on the blue Ionian water.

There are dolphins in the bay, sleek black backs breaking the surface, then rolling back under, only to reappear somewhere else. I watch the glittering sea like a hawk to see where.

Our house, the Villa La Buntessa, is one of only seven scattered among the wild grasses and giant eucalyptus trees of Contrada Limarra. Nothing will ever be built here again. It's just us and the turtle, protected by both EU and Italian law.

In fact nothing ever changes anyway hereabouts. In all the years we've been coming here we always return to the exact same everything. While the pace of change accelerates throughout the rest of the overcrowded world in, to me, increasingly alarming and disturbing ways, here in the tiny commune of Palizzi time stands reassuringly still. Some call it 'abbandonato'. I call it paradise.

The beach is usually deserted, and even in Luglio/Agosto the holidaymakers are few, none of them tourists, all of them Italian. No English voices except ours are ever to be heard in this neck of the woods, 'further off the beaten track than most people want to go' as

Bunty puts it. We are hard to find and harder still to get to. Public access is not encouraged, either by us residents or by the Comune di Palizzi. We are the number one habitat in all of Italy for the turtle – 'tartaruga', and the beach is UNESCO protected, as is the bay. We are a little lost world.

The bay is teeming with fish, small tuna, swordfish and sardine, and may only be fished by the small local fishing boats, lovely old traditional wooden craft, probably not much different to that of Phlebas the Phoenician, a long time dead.

Unique cross-currents flow through the Straits of Messina, ancient home of Scylla and Charybdis, and across the Ionian sea from Greece and Africa, bringing with them crystal-clear water and our ultra-sunny microclimate.

But this heavenly stretch of coast I found is a paradoxical one, a Paradiso con il diavolo, an Et in Arcadia Ego kind of place. There are many problemi. For example:

I arrived two days ago from London, on Alitalia, via the usual seven-hour wait in Rome airport, getting up in the morning at five and finally trundling up the slope into the Aeroporto del Stretto Reggio Calabria at six thirty p.m. It is 'troppo lontano' to get here, far too far for weekends or even half-term, and expensive. No direct flights to Ibiza are we.

Pasquale was there to meet me; silver hair and a suntan; big smile:

'EEEEEEE AN!' (Here I am Eeeeean or Yan or occasionally Ivan.)

'Come andiamo?'

'Pasquale!'

We did the kissing thing.

Anywhere else in the world Pasquale would probably be prime minister or something. He is a man of infinite resource. Here he ekes out a living hand to mouth, taking whatever lavoro he can get. Looking after Villa La Buntessa is probably his only regular employment, if you can call it that.

'E tu?' I said. 'Tutto bene?'

He shrugged in what you might call the Full Italian way as we headed across the hot (wonderfully hot) Aeroporto del Stretto parking lot to our old blue Fiat Multipla, Macchina Nostra. So called because it's mine as I paid for it, and his because it's registered in his name. In Italy, unlike every other European country, you have to be Italian to own a vehicle. Why this is so no one knows. It makes no sense, but then in Italy, especially in the south, very little does. Its Byzantine legal system is like one vast Jarndyce v Jarndyce rumbling interminably and pointlessly on, keeping armies of avvocati busy, and providing work for countless document-stamping bureaucrats in a land where real work, of the honest and productive kind, is extremely hard to come by.

I used to drive down from London in our ancient Toyota people carrier, loaded to the gunwales with goods from Ikea and Portobello Road, a three-day journey that eventually took too great a toll on both self and car. One time a leaky radiator had me filling it up every twenty minutes all the way from Dijon – a severe test of the nervous system. But it was a near miss with a lorry in Umbria, at the end of a fourteen-hour drive (it nearly was The End), that finally decided me to throw in the towel and quit the long-haul system.

Quite frankly I'm too old, my reactions are shot, and there's a lot of hard road en route, especially the Naples to Reggio A3, the so-called 'Autostrada del Sole', where unexpected hazards, much as they do in Calabria generally, suddenly overtake one and threaten to overwhelm. There are just too many steep mountain climbs in one coned-off lane behind grindingly slow (barely moving at all) lorries.

The A3, it was once explained to me, has a zero maintenance budget, rendering it not really an autostrada at all, but at least it's toll-free. And if there ever is any money allocated by the powers-that-be in Rome, it tends to go to contractors notoriously affiliated with such organisations as the Camorra of Naples and the 'Ndrangheta of Calabria, whose priorities almost certainly do not include the smooth flow of traffic through their southern fiefdoms.

We stowed the bags and climbed into the warm, scented interior – scented in the way that all Latino-operated cars seem to be. A saint bobbed reassuringly on the dashboard.

When we got onto the SS 106 I said, 'So – Pasquale, che fai?'

'Grandi problemi,' he replied, never one for beating about the bush.

My heart sank, not for the first time and certainly not for the last. That's the thing about coming down here, you never know what body blow is going to fall next. It's the unavoidable Death's Head in Arcady.

Is it all worth it financially? Has one at least made a good investment? Property tends to go up in value, especially beach property, but sadly not hereabouts I discovered, where people are either scared off by the mafia, or can't get here because of the impossible journey and the fact that there is zero tourist infrastructure if they do.

Pasquale and I once discussed 'valore di casa', and he simply pointed at the deserted beach and said 'valore la'. The real value is being non-existent on any estate agent's map, a kind of locational black hole in otherwise highly desirable Italy.

But there's much more to it than that. The beautiful empty beach is just a part of it. There's the whole southern Italian thing that first drew Bunty and me and keeps on drawing us; the people, for a start: warm like the sun, poor, laughing, happy, friendly, for whom chronic historic hardship has evolved into a sense of humour that strangely matches my own. Very few things aren't a huge joke. I felt it from the start, way beyond mere empathy. It's Theatre of the Absurd writ large. An Irish friend said it sounds like the west of Ireland only hot.

You can sit all day in the piazza bar drinking a one-euro cappuccino and watch the world go by with all the old retired mafiosi-looking guys, dripping with bling, leaning their chins on their sticks and chuckling over their grappa and limoncello. It's the Dolce Vita Calabrese and it isn't going anywhere; it isn't changing any time soon. You can buy pizza by the metre that's crunchy every centimetre of the way and the gelato is like nowhere else on Earth. Another Calabrese friend once described it to me as 'a paradise of nothing'.

So – what was it this time? I braced myself.

'Grandi problemi con casa di legno.'

'Casa di legno – oh no!'

The casa di legno, our lovely wooden garden house, I should explain, has been fraught with many problemi right from the start. When we first found the property Bunty and I both thought something might be done with the large vacant space at the back between the gates and the garage. The professore next door, we noticed, had a caravan in his garden, and she thought that might be a good idea.

I agreed with her until Pasquale's cousin Gianni got involved. He had a better idea, bigger and better and just as legal as a caravan – a house made of wood: a casa di legno. And of course it would involve far more lavoro for him and Pasquale. Just how much more I could never have imagined.

He showed me a brochura of these dwellings and they were indeed belle if not bellissime. I agreed they would be far superior to a caravan, and very soon after that Gianni's 'collega' Domenico was produced, a glib and convincing BMW driver from the historic mountain town of Serra San Bruno.

Collega is an imprecise term (most Calabrian terms are) I was to hear often, somewhere between a cousin and a friend, but not exactly either. Less baggage of personal responsibility attaches to a collega if things go wrong. And things did go very wrong indeed with Domenico.

'Sentenza di Tribunale per demolizione di casa di legno.'

They wanted me to knock down my beautiful wooden house. After all these years.

'Demolizione impossible, Pasquale – no! I have a condono!'

'Condono niente.'

'Si, si, Pasquale – I HAVE A CONDONO!'

'Architetto Napoli ditte me condono niente.'

The condono system, a brainwave of Signor Berlusconi, takes advantage of the fact that since all building work in Italy is illegal, an opportunity can be provided for offenders to wipe the slate clean by paying their local comune a whacking fee, in our case, in Palizzi,

100 euros per square metre, to 'condone' their illegal works and make them legal.

I had paid a hundred times 52 square metres equalling 5,200 euros many years back, and I had, I hoped, the paperwork somewhere or other to prove it.

When we got home I began to search. And miraculously my deep-seated memory, driven perhaps by desperation, led me unerringly to the spot, right at the back of a drawer in my mother's desk, where the four crucial slips of paper, eached signed and stamped by both the architetto and the comune, lay.

I rushed out waving them: 'Prove! Prove!'

Pasquale did actually seem impressed that I could be right and everybody else apparently wrong. We got back in the Fiat and headed at breakneck speed (Pasquale's preferred pace anyway) for the offices of architetto Napoli.

He was still open. I waved my bits of paper, proving beyond doubt that my beautiful wooden house had been condoned, and indeed that he had been instrumental in achieving it.

He raised his hands to heaven, then delved in an ancient-looking wooden cabinet where he soon found the file. Sure enough, there it was, the Condono di Comune di Palizzi. We were saved.

Only we weren't. An animated discussion between him and Pasquale, too rapid and 'dialetto' for me to follow, produced the following dismal prognosis:

Even though I had a condono, it was rendered null and void by the fact that the avvocato from Spropoli, far from winning as she had claimed, had abandoned the case nine years ago. The Comune di Palizzi had issued the condono on entirely false information. We had all, the architetto included, believed her.

The tribunale meanwhile, after waiting ten years for someone to turn up and defend the vigile's denunciation, had finally lost patience and delivered the sentenzo di demolizione, a sentence for which not only was there now no appeal, but one that would never have been delivered in the first place nine years ago. At the time such harsh judgements were unheard of, before the EU came along and stuck their oar in.

'Abandoned the case,' I said, sitting limply on the edge of a desk.

The architetto, his assistant and Pasquale all raised their hands in synchronised resignation, smiling and shaking their heads in stoic unison.

'But I paid her 480 euros. It was all tutto bene.'

'But it was not,' said the architetto, as if this explained everything. Their smiles became sadder and more philosphical.

'And what does she have to say about it?'

'She is matta.' It was the only explanation. The woman was mad, and sadly no one had realised it; crazy in the head. Actually, I had always suspected it.

And now what was to be done?

The head-shaking became more final; more in tune with the Calabrian doom-laden world view. There is no appeal against the might of the tribunale. I had one month to knock it down.

I left the building with Pasquale in a state of shock. The wooden house, over the years, had become weathered into its lovely cottage garden and surrounding foliage of bamboo, cypressas and flowering oleander, its veranda cool and shady, its interior colourful and comfortable. Years of trouble had eventually evolved into a jewel in the Buntessa crown. Everybody loved it, and it was a great favourite with our regular renters in July and August.

We drove back through the steep and narrow Palizzi streets to Pasquale's house where I would leave him, and where evening life was just getting into languid Italian swing in the little bright front flower gardens and overhanging balconies. Young ragazze and ragazzi strolled, or whizzed about on their mopeds, helmetless and carefree. How I envied them.

Pasquale's own balconia, on street level, was crowded with eager welcoming faces poised to greet me: his wife Melina, various sorelle and aunts, and Pasquale's grandson Pasquallino, or Pasquale Piccolo as I call him. He is a mad keen Chelsea supporter, and the fact that I technically live in Chelsea added extra fervour to his rush to embrace me, as he always does, hugging my legs with enthusiasm. 'Yan! Yan!'

He was in full Chelsea strip, and no amount of explaining that I support QPR ever has the slightest impact. I gave him a blue cap with 'Football' embroidered across the peak in white. It could after all relate to either team.

'Hey Pasquallino!' I said. 'Come?'

'Bene bene bene!'

Melina came forward and we embraced. 'Come stai?'

'Non cento percento bene, Melina,' I said. 'Grandi problemi con la mia casa di legno.'

'No! No, no – tranquillo, Ian.'

'Si si si, Melina – catastrofe.'

'Non è una catastrofe – Pasquale la risolvera!'

I looked at Pasquale hopefully. He shrugged and smiled.

'La risolvera?' I said.

'Non lo so possibile.'

Melina said, 'Tranquillo, Ian – Pasquale la risolvera.'

I cheered up. This was true, he would sort it out. He'd pulled off some spectacular rescues over the years. 'Si si, sempre risolvera lui. Pasquale – Grande Maestro di Risolvera.' I put my arm around his shoulder and hugged him.

Pasquale smiled inscrutably, 'Speriamo!'

Before I took possession of my old Fiat Multipla and left, there was one more thing: Pasquale's younger son Vincenzo was at last getting married to his long-term fidanzata, the bravissima ragazza Antonella. Saturday was to be his stag night.

'Probabilmente sedici amici, tutti maschi, venti al massimo.'

I didn't get it at first.

'Sei libero Sabato sera?' he asked.

Of course I was free. I am pretty well always libero. That's one of the big attractions of my paradise of nothing. I have managed to stop the world and get off.

I got it that Pasquale was inviting me. 'Si, Pasquale, sono sempre libero.' It did seem mildly surprising. We are friendly of course, but I am hardly one of Vincenzo's intimate buddies.

'E casa tua? Sempre libero?'

Now I got it. The penny dropped at last. Young and Calabrese though I may not be, I did at least possess the ideal venue.

'Solo barakka con grande tavola, y possibile barbecue?'

It is a venue which without Pasquale I could not possibly continue to enjoy. His commitment to it is equal to my own, and he knows much more about keeping it going than I do. He loves the place, and when I'm not there he goes on loving it. It's not far off being Casa Nostra in much the same way as the Multipla is Macchina Nostra.

There was no way I could refuse. Anyway I was happy to host Vincenzo's stag do. We discussed some of the details, there was a lot more embracing all round, and finally I climbed aboard the good old Multipla and tootled off, very much the popular padrone, grateful arriverdercis from everyone ringing in my ears.

Next day I did the rounds in Palizzi, and was greeted by all and sundry with great enthusiasm. I must say I enjoy these homecomings. Palizzi is home to some twelve hundred souls all of whom know and/or are related to each other and all of whom know me now after so many years. I am no longer a complete outsider though still something of a curiosity – the Inglese, the only one they've ever seen.

Nowhere else I've ever been is everyone so friendly. You don't pass people by on the street in Palizzi without a salve, or a buongiorno, buonasera, come stai? etc. People throughout the ages have dreamed of utopias, but for my money Palizzi is hard to beat, a microcosom of southern Italian life. The very old and the very young and everyone in between are looked after for life in what amounts to one large family. Introspection and loneliness are kept at bay by a way of life that's outdoor and outward and communal rather than indoor and inward. It's impossible to 'isolate' in a place like this. Old age and loneliness are a major problem elsewhere but not here. Poverty is not a problem either because everyone is poor.

In the scale of what people look for architecturally in little Italian towns it scores about a zero, but it gets ten out of ten in my book for the culture that lives rather than the kind you look at in guide books: life as it is lived by Italians here and now.

In the hills above lies its medieval counterpart Palizzi Superiore, complete with eleventh-century Norman castle and surrounded by the hardy mountain vineyards that make Palizzi a 'Città del Vino'. If you want more of an aesthetic fix and you're prepared to rough it over the steep potholed hairpin-bended horrors of the road for eleven kilometres uphill, then Old Palizzi is the place for you. There's a fourth-century Byzantine chapel nearby, used at present to house goats.

But there's nothing to do when you get there and nowhere to stay. You can't get into the castle (the Barone lives in Reggio and keeps it locked), so really the most you can hope for is the journey back. The relief on getting down to sea level again makes the whole thing worth it. You can sit outside the piazza bar and reflect on life in the mountains, and what on earth that must be like in winter.

I saved my visit to the supermercato to last, partly so as not to lug my shopping around in the heat, but also because the welcome there is always the warmest. Ernesto, who speaks a little English after a stint in the oil business in Saudi Arabia, and his family, the signora, two large sons and one daughter, always treat me like some sort of prodigal son whose return from the remote outer world becomes a greater and greater event with every passing year.

'Good-a-MORning,' says the tubby and beaming Ernesto as soon as he sees me. 'And how are-a YOU today? You have-a been a-swimming in the mare?' The fact that I live on the beach makes this inevitable of course. 'Non ha troppo freddo?'

It is actually a bit freddo in May, and anyway I hadn't had time to get round to it, or down to it, the beach being a bit bassa this year and too great a leap from my gate without Pasquale supervising his invaluable sidekick Michele in some much-needed sand-shovelling.

'Adesso no,' I said apologetically, 'probabilmente dopo.' A lot of things in Calabria are probabilmente dopo. It was an answer to which Ernesto could easily relate.

Palizzi being a celebrated 'Città del Vino', and Ernesto its leading retailer, he is a very great expert on wine. Upon my telling him of tomorrow's great event at my house, the stag do of Vincenzo, which he already knew all about, he hurried me over to the vino section, where I had intended buying a token bottle of Prosecco.

'No, no, no!' Ernesto positively exploded with the word. 'No! He will *only* want champagne! I think that only this very fine bottle of Moët and Chandon will do for such a festa as you are planning for him so generously at your house!'

An Inglese such as myself, in other words, would surely not want to spoil the ship for a ha'pth of tar.

I added it to my basket. It was ten times the price of Prosecco.

The following evening I was primed and ready for anything. The bottle of Moët was chilling in the fridge. The same could not be said for myself. I paced about nervously.

At seven o'clock there was a loud racket at the top of the drive, and two laden flatbed trucks came clattering down and parked next to the barbecue. I was glad to see Pasquale in one of them.

Two beefy buddies of his I didn't know piled out with him and started unloading. I greeted them all but was soon politely sidelined. I retreated to my veranda – running the risk of seeming standoffish to be comfortable – and sat there watching the show.

It was pretty interesting. My sturdy twelve-year-old barbecue, not much more than stacked slabs of cement, was transformed into a raging furnace by extending its height and placing a huge piece of flat metal on top which heated up to become a giant griddle capable of cooking a series – a continuous series – of courses for twenty hearty hungry Calabrese, plus myself. Fat fragrant olive-wood logs were piled on and fired up.

Bags of buns and sacks of steaks were offloaded, plus various pig products, bacon in particular, which sizzled with everything all evening, but also pork chops, ribs and steaks, and big circular floppy pizzas home-made by Melina.

Beer in great quantities was placed in various receptacles of mine, in particular my wheelbarrow, along with sacks of ice. Once this was done we were ready to rock and roll, and down the drive came the first of the revellers in their cars, horns blaring.

I rose from my veranda and prepared to mingle. I cast about for anyone I knew but came up empty apart from Vincenzo himself, his brother Domenico, and Pasquale, who, on this occasion, was far too busy to perform his usual protective services for the grande padrone Inglese.

Everyone soon headed for our long family table, which inhabits a charming al fresco dining area alongside the barakka, under a canopy of bamboo and bougainvillea. It is quite capable of seating twenty or more, and Pasquale hurried around collecting chairs.

Everyone took their places like clockwork, as if pre-arranged, leaving me dithering to and fro, desperately seeking someone I could spend the next several hours beside. Once the Calabrese get heated up, which they were already doing, my conversational abilites plummet from piccolo to niente. Their words rattle out impossibly fast, and the dialetto becomes impossibly broad: the whole thing runs together like a completely different language.

Suddenly I felt myself being lifted from behind, off my feet, and plonked down in the middle of the row, distressingly centre-stage, the last place I would have chosen.

The perpetrator of this outrage sat down next to me. It was Domenico, Pasquale's older son, brother of Vincenzo and father of Pasquale Piccolo. His wife is a Polish girl called Yvonne, and it was she who once described the Calabrese to me in the immortal words 'drive fast – everything else slow'.

Domenico is something of a black sheep, large and shaggy and rough, a throwback to ancient times when the Vandals conquered Africa, and the legions marched this way to Sicily, staining the soil with blood, in a series of vain attempts to win back the bread basket of the Empire.

He gave me a bear hug that almost pulled me off my chair, and tried to aim a wine bottle into my glass of Sprite. 'Salute, Yan – vino di Calabria.' It's a well-known fact that I don't drink, one that's taken me years to get them to accept. Quitting is not a concept they find easy to relate to. I shook my head, 'Grazie, no.'

Speaking of bread baskets, one now began doing the rounds, and I was glad of the distraction, whereby cramming my mouth with what has been called 'distressful bread' I was able to converse unintelligibly without it being too noticeable.

This device proved extremely effective throughout the meal, and could be employed on a variety of mastications, bacon, beefsteak, more bread, pork ribs, pork chops, more bacon, Melina's pizza, yet more bread, until I was so full that, for perhaps the first time in my life I was literally unable to cram in one more morsel.

But by then the thing had become academic, as the Calabrese were way beyond noticing or caring about anything I was doing. The beer had done its work, and most of them had taken to horsing around on the barakka terrace, or rushing down to the beach and throwing each other into the sea.

All that remained, once they had cooled off, was the Grand Finale, for which everyone was by now very much in the mood. Pasquale officiated, while I hurried unseen to the house, reappearing at the moment of maximum impact to pop the cork off the Moët, swirl the streaming foaming contents into a row of plastic cups, take my bow, and join in the toasting and cheering, which included much Chelsea! Chelsea! Chelsea! in my honour, once more the popular padrone Inglese.

By midnight Pasquale had removed all trace, so in the morning one would never know that any such revelry had ever happened. As I wandered down to the barakka terrace with my first caffè Inglese of the day it might all have been a dream.

Which brings me back to my dolphin-watching reverie, seated under Stumpy the olive tree (so named by Bunty when she first saw it), sipping my coffee, gently recovering from the night before, and wondering, not for the first time or the last, how on Earth I'd landed up in this precise spot, among these people, now like a second family.

What had motivated me? Was it all in fact destino? Meant to be? I couldn't imagine life without it. It would be simpler, certainly, but far less interesting. Calabria remains a paradox wrapped in a mystery, a still undiscovered world. What *was* it that brought me down here?

I can't really explain it, except to say that I felt moved to do so, the call of the wild you might say, and I thought I would find what I was looking for when I got there.

No one seemed to know much about the place, or even where it was exactly. The 'toe' and the 'boot' were mentioned quite a lot. Oh, and the mafia. One of those big fat Italy guide books said that if you were thinking of getting off the train anywhere between Naples and Reggio Calabria don't bother. I asked a lady at Thomas Cook about Italy's Ionian Sea coast, and she said there isn't one.

But in another guide book, *The Blue Guide*, I read that 'South of Locri there are miles of sandy beaches with no one on them'. How could that possibly be in Mediterranean Europe, let alone Italy? I studied my map in the Calabria book the Italian State Tourist Board had sent me (no English translation available). There it was – Locri. On the very Ionian coast the Thomas Cook lady had denied – the 'Jonica', with miles of sandy beaches, beyond the pale, apparently, of tourism. An opportunity, even in this day and age, to discover an unexplored region. I made up my mind to go there asap. It was called the Jasmine Coast. How romantic-sounding was that?

Europe's most colourful and least understood extremity appeals to the romantic spirit of adventure, and to a certain poetic longing to find answers to life's riddles in its darker, wilder, less 'civilised' places. For Calabria, Italian though it is, Greek and Roman though it was, remains stubbornly unconvinced about being European. It is poor and backward but rich in tradition. It is hot and lazy and sleepy and friendly. It is the Mezzogiorno. It refuses to be tamed or brought up to date even today, when tourism and television has ripped the mystery out of almost everywhere else on earth. It is mountainous and green – 'the lungs of Europe' – great spinal ranges cloaked in ancient forest, with a unique rural economy. There was never an industrial revolution here; perennially backward, permanently in recession.

In the footsteps of Edward Lear and other intrepid Englishmen I went, deep into the warm south, inspired by their discoveries in this still mysterious region, and by their luminous writings.

Diverse as they may have been as men, there is a common thread of inquisitive eccentricity which runs through all these great Calabrian travellers, who saw in southern Italy something splendid and majestic, comic and tragic, that was being missed by their Grand Tour contemporaries.

Far be it from me to compare myself to such as these. Nevertheless I hope my account may help to bring something of this 'Altro Mondo' to life for you, comfortable in your armchair and far from the many perils and vicissitudes that faced me.

2

Et in Calabria Ego

'Even in Arcady,' explains the great art historian Erwin Panofsky, 'I, Death, am present.' There is a twist to the Arcadian idyll. All is not necessarily as rosy as it seems.

I found this out for myself in Calabria. My friend Gianni says 'Paradiso con il diavolo', which comes to roughly the same thing: 'You can't have a paradise without a devil in it.' This is also a very Calabrese way of looking at things.

In fact Calabria *was* once Arcady, settled by the Arcadians long before the great Hellenic colonisations of the eighth century BC.

And later it was Italy. Italo, king of the Enotrians, grandson of Pelasgus, who came in 'very early times', probably around 2000 BC, from Arcadia, gave the name 'Italia' to Calabria long before it caught on and spread to the whole country. This is the Ancient World indeed.

These Enotrians, sons of Arcady, were the people the Hellenic colonisers found on their arrival, and promptly turned into serfs to till their land and build their magnificent cities, which at the height of the Hellenic Age were reputedly more splendid than Athens itself.

From Arcadia to serfdom! And now those proud Hellenes themselves, the present-day Calabrese, are looked down on in their turn by the Italians of the north, superior in their splendid Renaissance cities to what they see as the rustic and backward south – the Mezzogiorno.

Little now remains of the glory that was Greater Greece: Magna Graecia. Those glittering city-states destroyed each other in their perpetual pursuit of war. Now there are only sad museums in places like Locri, the first ever city-state to have written laws, once the Jewel of the Mediterranean when Rome was still just a village.

✳

I stumbled on our particular Angolo di Paradiso while searching for somewhere that hadn't been concreted over and infested with Easyjetters, where the old Mediterranean life still lingered. Impossible, you might say.

My goal was the Ionian Sea coast of Calabria, gateway to the Eastern Mediterranean and all the romance of the Ancient World, inspired by retracing George Gissing's journey in *By the Ionian Sea*, as well as by Lear's *Journals of a Landscape Painter in Southern Calabria*, and the incomparable *Old Calabria* of Norman Douglas, perhaps the greatest travel book ever written.

In 1901 or thereabouts Gissing travelled on 'The Seaside Line', a single-track railway running down the Ionian coast of Magna Graecia to Reggio Calabria, originally Asteniti, the ancient city by the sea founded by Noah's grandson Ashkenaz soon after the waters of the Great (albeit mythical) Flood receded.

And lo! The Seaside Line is still there. Independent as ever from the Italian State Railway, winding unfenced through fields, charming as ever to someone who finds railway tracks romantic, who as a boy used to put pennies on the line at Dartmouth Harbour, where the mighty steam locos of the Devon Belle used to roll into Kingswear, and wait for them to be squashed into burnished copper pancakes.

But I didn't travel on it, choosing instead to track it down by rented car from Brindisi. That way I thought I could explore more freely, and avoid some impossibly complicated Italian timetables.

✳

The adventure really began as soon as I stepped aboard my Alitalia flight to Rome. Rome! Not that you see much of the Eternal City in Fiumicino airport.

I'm one of only a handful of people who like Alitalia. So what if they nearly always lose your bags? The Italian Experience really begins once you board one of their (usually late) planes. It's all smiles and buongiornos from then on. Sadly they don't serve meals any more or even panini, but the coffee's good and sometimes there's a bag of biscotti (salati or dolci?), and once you do finally take off, it's only a couple of hours or so to Rome, to where all roads are said to lead.

Having landed and made my way along several miles of walkways to the Domestic Departures part of Rome airport, I tried my novice Italian – gleaned inflight from a phrase book I'd bought – on the disdainful barrista behind the bar near my gate.

He pretended to non capire, and I hadn't first bought a biglietto, but in the end, after a large crowd of increasingly interested parties had had their say, and pretty well everyone in the Domestic Departures lounge had become involved, I walked away triumphant.

Nothing ever tastes so good as that first truly Italian thing. And I felt that special rapport, one more example of the historic bond between the Roman and British Empires.

When the Emperor Claudius invaded Britain in AD 43, instead of simply trying to subdue it, he cunningly invited the sons of the chiefs to Rome for a taste of the Dolce Vita. They took to it like ducks to water, and it's been the same for Englishmen ever since.

Now it was my turn. No longer young, no longer technically a son, nor had my father been a chief exactly, more of a chief executive, nevertheless my own Grand Tour had begun.

And I was ready for it. Italian is largely a question of hand gestures. It's no good just speaking Italian; you have to *be* Italian. Tie an Italian's hands behind his back and he becomes mute. I tried to behave accordingly.

The domestic flight to Brindisi was more Italian than ever.

Everyone on board seemed to know each other, and I longed to be a part of it all. I nodded and smiled at what I thought were appropriate moments in many incomprehensible exchanges, until all too soon we were descending over the small palm-fringed harbour, with its handful of ships, bound, no doubt, for ports and inlets of Greek and Levantine romance. Thoughts of the Durrells sprang to mind: if only I could find somewhere to compare with their 1930s Corfu.

The airport was small and palm-fringed too, a bit like Palma Mallorca in the fifties, where I used to fly on hols with my parents by propellor-driven Vickers Viscounts. The sense of nostalgia was palpable.

Antonino, at the only car-rental place that didn't require a credit card, was very Italian indeed – dark and handsome, white shirt and teeth, Ray-Bans, of course – and spoke English.

'You will visit the beautiful baroque city of Lecce?'

'I was rather planning on driving straight down into Calabria.'

Antonino shrugs doubtfully, 'The city of Lecce is beautiful.'

I say, 'Calabria too is beautiful, I'm told.'

Antonino shrugs more profoundly, his palms raised heavenwards, his whole body and soul going into it: 'All of Italy is beautiful.'

I piled my stuff into my low-budget Punto, my home for the foreseeable future, and the adventure was on. ·

It was two p.m. and after diverse false starts (going the wrong way round my first Italian roundabout) I headed for the city of Taranto, gateway to the Jonica and all points south. I needed to get a move on.

I hadn't got the hang of Italian roads and the way they signed them – even now my heart is in my mouth most of the time. The great thing is not to get lost, because if you do your limited, in my case non-existent, Italian, will become a source of increasing confusion, and very likely drive you deeper and deeper into an impenetrable web. This is what happened to me at Taranto.

I'd made the mistake of coming off the superstrada – I don't know why exactly; I'd been thinking 'Taranto' for so long I suppose, that when I saw it signed I just went for it. Next thing I knew I was in a maze of smaller and smaller streets, none of which went anywhere I wanted to go. I could see my road far across the Gulf – how I longed to cross that sparkling water.

In despair I pulled into a filling station and began throwing myself on their mercy. They didn't understand English, but after a while the words 'Reggio Calabria' seemed to register with a very old man who up till then had been sitting on a bench smoking a cigarette and resting his chin on his stick. Suddenly he climbed into the car beside me.

'Vai, vai,' he said, more than a little peevishly.

This peevishness increased as we went along, him giving what I assumed were directions, me failing to understand them, other road users braking and hooting madly, the whole thing orchestrated by his stick, with which he kept trying to point the way, and which kept getting tangled up with the gear stick.

After a while we entered more tranquil waters, and seemed to be making our way through a semi-derelict residential area of half-finished, grey breeze-block flats typical of most Italian towns. I had by then got the hang of the words 'destra' and 'sinistra', but I was becoming more and more convinced that all he'd done was con me into giving him a lift home.

Then at the end of what I'd thought was a cul-de-sac, populated mainly by stray dogs and cats, my guide pointed excitedly ahead.

'Reggio! Reggio!' He got out and saluted me, 'Va bene.'

And sure enough, to my utter astonishment, there in this hinterland of nowhere, stuck against a grey breeze-block wall, was a beautiful blue sign with the magic words – SS 106.

I didn't get lost again till nightfall. I'd wanted to follow the coast road but got tricked in the dark onto the autostrada A3. They both said Reggio Calabria – a not unusual Italian conundrum.

Even in darkness I could tell I was heading inland, and at a speed far greater than I would wish. Italians drive fast. They come up behind you and flash their lights. You end up getting swept along, at higher and higher speeds, and if you happen to be in a panic anyway you soon lose your sense of pretty well everything: all you want to do is get off.

I got off the autostrada in what appeared to be the middle of nowhere. I thought wistfully of Neil Young ('Everybody knows this is…') and immediately realised how tired I was. I was a long way from Zuma Beach and anywhere else they speak English. I stopped and looked around: nothing.

As in life I suppose, according to Mr Micawber anyway, if you keep going long enough something will always turn up. Hopefully. Speriamo. Knowing I was too tired to drive, and probably too old for this sort of thing, spurred me on rather than stopped me. I'm not one of those people who can sleep in the car, least of all in the mafia-infested mountains of Calabria. Anxiety (fear, really) can become an energy when all your adrenalin is used up. I desperately needed to get there, wherever it was, asap.

Another thing that gets used up is petrol. Adventurers before me in these mysterious lands, like Gissing and Douglas and Lear and co., hardier than me no doubt, at least didn't have to worry about petrol. And they probably planned things better; at a horse's pace you can't go so wrong so fast.

But in those ancient hills that night, some pagan deity – Dionysus, Apollo? – was looking out for me. As the last drops of everything drained out of both me and my Punto, a small town appeared, and I freewheeled into a filling station, miraculously still open. Unlike the town's only hotel.

The Hotel Presidente stood, dark and imposing, behind some trees behind the filling station. The pump attendant said (hand gestures) it might be worth knocking. So I knocked on the big glass doors and rang the bell repeatedly, and after a while a light came on. A sleepy concierge appeared, pulling on a maroon uniform jacket.

He looked at me drowsily. 'Chiuso,' he said.

The word for tired is 'stanco'. I didn't know that then, but something in my pathetic manner got through to the human within the official, as perhaps it wouldn't have done with a member of most other nations. Italians, though they invented fascism, are the most human and humorous of races, and it doesn't usually take long before they start shaking their heads and smiling, the Calabrese more than most. Rules are made to be broken, especially in the south.

The air conditioning had been switched off, the windows were sealed shut and the September weather was still boiling, but I was welcome to any room I fancied for 30 euros. In large, oven-like luxury I passed out till morning.

I woke up in Calabria, full of hope and renewed energy. I had a headache, but had achieved at least part of my goal. I didn't know where I was, but I could always ask. Downstairs the concierge had cranked up the espresso machine and piled a plate with brioches and cornetti.

I was in Rogliano, on the wrong coast it turned out, but I decided to drive down it anyway for a while.

Looking at my map, the distance across became much narrower further down, and if I crossed via the mountain town of Serra San Bruno I would still come out on the Jonica north of Locri, south of which was where I was headed.

Why was I headed there? What had motivated this seemingly eccentric impulse? It was hard to explain, but easy to explain to Bunty, the one person who is always ready for anything, and despite repeated unexpected setbacks always able to see the silver lining. She married me after all, an outsider if ever there was one.

Bunty had just endured a five-year cabin-cruiser obsession of mine, which cost a fortune. She is not a boat-lover; not one of those grey wives in anoraks you see braving the ocean wave while their husband splices the main brace. In fact she dislikes boats. Yet, here we were again, but at least the latest project was on terra firma.

To quote Winston Churchill (who once dandled the infant Bunty on his knee) and say I was 'walking with Destiny', wouldn't and shouldn't be enough for most wives. But Bunty is different. She has a way of squaring up to whatever's next with fortitude and humour. I suppose it's really a romantic nature, which despite all the dictates of common sense still soldiers on. That and the shared hope of a holiday home, on a beach, large enough for our enormous family (twenty-three in all). We discussed it and both decided that Calabria was a good bet, outside all the odds as it was, and for that reason perhaps affordable on our (very) limited budget.

'I will know it when I find it,' I assured her.

And Mediterranean men do seem to grow old in a good way, brown and smiling to the last, weathered like walnuts, puttering about on Vespas piled with sacks of olives. Like Nelson before me, I would be an 'Old Mediterranean Man'.

And I had an idea that if I could only make contact with the Ancient World, my soul might travel to the mythical Isles of the Hesperides, which I'm certain are somewhere nearby in the Ionian Sea, in the vicinity of Scylla and Charybdis. Without my boat I wasn't sure how I'd reach them, but I hoped that from the right spot on shore I could project myself into a mystical voyage and merge my essential being into an idyllic future in the Ancient Past.

Driving with Destiny, therefore, I made my way down the disappointing Tyrrhenian coast. It wasn't at all what I was looking for: mile after mile of apartment buildings and railway tracks – nothing to write home about; no nostalgic niches passed over by the juggernaut of progress.

At long last I headed into the hills. Calabria, despite its thousand kilometres of coast, is a mountainous country of mountain people. Ninety-four per cent of its towns are in the mountains. Only recently has the coast become hospitable. Saracens and malarial mosquitoes and a lack of natural harbours has kept the Calabrese largely inland for 2,500 years, from the Hellenic Age to the Second World War, when the chemist Paul Müller at last discovered the use of DDT.

A vast green land opened up: soaring mountains and deep gorges, and narrow country lanes winding through medieval villages. Higher and higher we went, my low-budget Punto and me, until the deep forests of pine gave way to deciduous trees, and the air, baking on the coast, smelt fresh and chill.

People stared as we went past, old women sweeping their steps and old men sitting outside bars: in their timeless changeless world almost anything is a novelty. Quaint enough in the sunlight, but what goes on up here in the long winter evenings, year after year, I wondered? I shuddered to think. The truth was, I wanted time to have stood still for me, but I didn't want to end up trapped in it like these folk, however picturesquely.

Winding down the other side, through orchards and vineyards, olive groves and villages, I glimpsed the fabled Ionian at last, in snapshots through gaps at first, then spread out before me like the promise of a miracle foretold, gold sparks dancing and glittering on an impossible shimmering sheet of blue, until it merged with the heartbreaking blueness of the sky. Stout Cortez himself, silent upon that peak in Darien, could not have felt more filled with awe and wonder than me. If I'd felt doubts about the wisdom of my journey, they were dispelled as I descended to that ancient and magical shore.

The difference was immediate: not the majestic drama of the Amalfi coast – far from it – and definitely not everyone's cup of tea. But for me, I could feel my senses responding at once. Miles of coast-land – flat, even monotonous – the road rolling on without much variety, but it was the very emptiness that appealed to me. A few small towns, architecturally unimpressive and even ugly, then more long straight stretches of sandy beach, wide and empty, sometimes obscured by pines, sometimes by enormous stands of wild cane, but hardly ever by buildings. Virgin isn't the right word for something so raggedy; unspoilt is wrong too – this was no South Sea Island, but it was wild – wild and free and empty. And beyond the beach that blue, unbearably romantic sea, stretching away to the shores of Greece and Africa.

To my right the hills sloped gently down in a patchwork of fields and orchards, often marred at the roadside by ugly buildings, but all somehow unobtrusive and 'undeveloped' – no serried ranks of grotty apartment blocks here. The landscape was winning, crowned by an occasional ruined Saracen or Norman castle.

The seaside towns I passed through were bustling and nondescript, laid out to please no one but themselves; red breeze-block showing through unfinished plaster on balconies draped with washing; fruit stands out on the sidewalk buzzing with flies; nothing for the aesthete to gasp over; nothing for the tourist because there aren't any.

Siderno (upmarket shops and restaurants), Locri (once a fabled Greek city-state), then Bovalino (incongruously modern shopping mall) and Bianco (home of 'The Best Gelateria in the World').

Heading out of Bianco I felt my pulse quicken: I was almost as far south as I could go now and the landscape was changing in subtle ways. We weren't going in a dead straight line any more; at Capo Sant'Anna dense groves of olive and citrus, laced with tiny lanes, ran down to the sea, following an invisible river. Then, after Africo Nuovo (reputedly our local mafia stronghold), the road ran uphill to the point at which I really felt I'd found what I was searching for: a giant headland bent the road round to the west, and the full panorama of the Jasmine Coast was spread below me.

I would have stopped the car if I could (there's always someone on your tail in Italy). A beach of impossible size and beauty stretched away, like Malibu must have been before the moguls came, until it disappeared from view around another headland. Wide empty land, golden sloping hillsides where the apartment blocks should have been but weren't; how could such a place possibly exist in modern mainland Europe – in Italy, no less?

At Ferruzzano some effort had been made to capitalise on the long wide white beach: a road was built beside it for a short way, dotted with unkempt palms. Some RVs were parked, complete with satellite TV dishes. Further along were four or five spectacular beach houses, close together and obviously built years ago. Some rich Italians from the north must have discovered this beach before me; but it clearly hadn't caught on: beyond them the beach reverted to its virgin state, and continued like that for several kilometres to Brancaleone.

The road wound through wide, open country; hay bales rolled on gently sloping hillsides, reminiscent of harvest time in Tuscany, and the gleaming single track of the Seaside Line wound beside it.

The feeling of Destino, which I've never been able to properly explain, peaked in Brancaleone.

Brancaleone wasn't that different from previous seaside towns, yet it is. (I suppose they all are when you get to know them.) It seemed extra bustling, with a definite holiday atmosphere. Some sort of festival was going on, and it made me feel welcome, almost as if I'd been expected. I just needed to keep my eyes skinned and my reward would be revealed: I would know it when I saw it. I was getting close.

Sure enough, just after Capo Spartivento, the very next village, a little bay appeared, a sickle of sand with a couple of fishing boats drawn up; and through the pine and eucalyptus around the shore something white twinkled – something I had to take a closer look at.

But there was no road. I knew there must be a way down, but for the life of me I couldn't find it. Three times I ended up in Spropoli, the next village, and three times I had to turn round, watched by the increasingly interested villagers. I tried asking them, but they just shook their heads and stared at this alien Inglese.

Driving back for the third time I pulled off the road to take stock. I couldn't think straight in this constant gyration, and there was a patch of waste ground by the roadside where I decided to stop and get my head together.

I realised then that the hand of destiny was indeed upon me, for the waste ground was really the opening to a sandy track, invisible from the road, which sloped down under the road bridge over which I'd just driven.

Under the bridge we went, and under the Seaside Line railway bridge next to it. I later learned it was called the Bridge of the White Nightingale.

I had descended into a different world. I switched off the engine. All I could hear was birdsong, and the breeze in the treetops, and the hush of small waves on the beach ahead. A little river trickled by over its stony bed. I started up again and drove on, and fifty yards later parked on white sand under some pines. The smell of the sea hit me as I opened the door. I stepped out onto the beach.

3

The Pinos

I crunched across the sand to the water's edge and stared out to sea. I put my hands on my hips and breathed in, drinking deeply of ozone and satisfaction; here I was, and here, somehow, I must remain. I looked along the length of the gently curving bay: a white lighthouse stood above the point at Spartivento. There wasn't a soul in sight. I raised my hands in salutation; if Agamemnon had rowed into view at that moment I shouldn't have been surprised.

Leaving the car where it was I started off in the direction of the lighthouse. I hadn't gone far when I saw my first sign of human habitation: some rough steps had been constructed out of railway sleepers, with ripe prickly pears growing either side. At the top of the steps a wooden door was set into a wall. It was slightly ajar.

For the second time in under an hour I entered a different world. Mounting the steps and gently easing the door, I found myself in a tiled courtyard of what at first seemed Moorish splendour. I'd seen similar in Spain and California's Santa Barbara, but here, in what I'd thought Crusoeland, it seemed shockingly incongruous.

How I struck it, or rather the inhabitants of it, was equally a shock. Two small boys looked up from whatever they were doing and promptly fled into the house.

For some reason I took them to be American; they were far fairer than the dark Calabrese I'd seen so far, and I think my addled brain was making a connection between this courtyard and those in California where I'd lived on a very different beach.

I called out in English. 'Hello! Anyone at home?'

So far my appearance hadn't seemed important, mostly a matter between myself and my car: I wore my old blue-checked chef's trousers, which had become considerably rumpled, and a torn Hawaiian shirt. (Chef's trousers are cheap and cheerful, and you can buy them from catering suppliers, thus avoiding the horrors of menswear shops with their tight, claustrophobic changing cubicles. And they have one-size-fits-all elasticated waistbands.)

The boys were not American, but Italian, and as such, even at their tender age, sensitive to sartorial issues. It's hardly surprising they ran away from an interloper dressed as I was: a beach bum, or 'vagabondo', or worse.

They fetched their mother to see for herself the horror that had come upon them. I introduced myself as best I could. Once it transpired I was an Inglese, she seemed relieved. Inglesis are a virtually unknown species down here, so they might very well look like me.

She invited me to sit under the veranda, where the boys, Dario and Davide, had their drawing books spread on a long wooden table, while she went indoors to make coffee.

Celeste was my first friend in Calabria and, as it turned out, I couldn't have asked for a better one. The way I found her that day, in that inaccessible place, me from my world and she from hers, has always seemed to both of us a prize example of Destino.

She is a sweet-natured person, and this quality has spread throughout her family. The boys, once the initial shock had worn off, couldn't wait to befriend me. Davide in particular, every time he looked at me, burst out laughing, and it's still the same today. He can't get over it.

They showed me their books and told me all about everything, in the most open and unselfconscious way, quite unlike shy English children inhibited by middle-class decorum. Not that they didn't have the most perfect manners: minus the curiosity, this was in part an expression of that, welcoming the stranger within their gates. Southern Italians are far more mannered than us and everything is done with a certain formalised ritual. High fives and casualness have not replaced the formal greeting, the handshake, the embrace, the kiss on both cheeks, the words of polite enquiry after the health of greetee and family, even among the young. This ritualisation gives a kind of baroque theatricality to life in the 'Altro Mondo', old-fashioned, structured and reassuring, like Celeste automatically making coffee for me.

When it came, we settled down to a conversation about what on earth I was doing there. How we conducted it I can't recall or explain, but with her few English words and my zero Italian we somehow covered it, to the point of my saying 'You are living in my Dream. This is what I'm searching for, something exactly like this, on this very beach.'

She laughed and shook her head.

'Impossible,' she said.

'Some land for sale, maybe?' Again she shook her head. It was a very small place and anyway you can't build on it.

We chatted some more. I was reluctant to leave, hoping for a miracle, enjoying just being there. Finally I knew I had to go, and with a sinking heart bade my new amici farewell. The idea that I would probably never see them again seemed unbearable, just as it did, driving slowly and reluctantly back up the sandy track, to leave forever this Garden of Eden where I, for so brief a spell, was a visitor in Elysium.

It was lucky I drove slowly. My reluctance paid off. Just as I reached the bend under the bridge, which would take me out of Arcady forever, and back to the real world, I glanced in my driving mirror for a last look. There in my dust were Dario and Davide, running and waving and yelling 'Fermati!'

I didn't need to know the meaning of the word to get their meaning, and I didn't need telling twice. Like Dick Whittington I turned around, the boys piled in and we headed back to paradise.

During my brief absence Celeste had phoned her husband, Pino. He had agreed for her to tell me what she'd known all along, that yards away from where we sat there was, indeed, something for sale. She explained that she'd told him I was a 'brava persona' – a 'good person', something I've felt under a slight strain to live up to since. Into their closed and secret world I had somehow managed to be admitted.

We set off up the beach for a viewing, the boys frisking about excitedly, me in the early stages of a dream state from which I was not to emerge for some time. This couldn't really be happening.

After a short walk, we stood on the sand before large locked gates, where a big old twisted tree spread its branches over a funky tin shanty-shack – somewhere between a caravan and a Chinese pagoda. A showerhead on a pipe stood beside the tree.

'Bellissima,' I said: Jamaica meets Malibu on the Jasmine Coast.

It was so perfect I didn't worry too much about how all our twenty-three persone would fit into it. My only worry was quanto costa.

This worry was magnified when Celeste beckoned me to continue. The shanty-shack was only for starters; on offer was nothing short of a beach estate. We followed the fenced sea wall for a hundred metres or more, until we arrived at house number three, number two being the villa itself, set back behind a wide tangle of vegetation. Number three was the boathouse.

Signor Tralongo, the Sicilian vendor, was a keen fisherman, and the sea here teems with fish. The boathouse had big wooden doors, which opened directly onto the sand, allowing egress for a large fishing boat, via its winch equipment inside.

In other words, the thing was getting more and more over the top, more what my mother liked to call 'a rich man's toy' – her way of reminding me I was pretty well permanently broke, whereas my father had been rich, and I couldn't afford 'toys' like Rolls Royces, yachts and a house in Spain like him.

When he died she inherited what was left of his millions, the idea being that the residue would trickle down to my sister and me on her demise. But when she died she did the dirty and cut me out of her will, a state of affairs only remedied when my sister very decently cut me in again.

Once the government took their cut (most of it) there wasn't much change for rich men's toys like beach estates. I'd found what I was looking for, only, yet again it seemed, beyond my means. I wondered if the shanty-shack could somehow be bought separately.

I left it that we would reconvene on the morrow, and that Pino would do all he could to bring Signor Tralongo along.

Having been embraced fondly by all three, I made my way back to the real-life highway and started thinking about somewhere to stay. I hadn't noticed any hotels, and naturally assumed there must be some closer to Reggio. There weren't and it took me a hot hour and a half to find out, as the urban sprawl of Reggio reached out to disillusion me.

As I hurried back to Spropoli and the vicino I'd now come to regard as home, the magic of my morning began to reassert itself. If I couldn't find a hotel I would sleep on the beach.

In Capo Spartivento (also known as Galati) I spotted a place to park where a well-worn path crossed the railway track onto the beach. I struggled out of my outer garments in the car, and in my boxer shorts headed for my first baptismal submersion in the magical waters of the Ionian.

This anointing was not a disappointment. As the warm silky sea closed over me I felt cleansed and reborn. This will sound fanciful I know, but there, on that quiet, sunny, September evening in Galati, a good chunk of my Anglo-Saxon uptightness was washed away, and in my heart and soul I became mezzo-Calabrese. I didn't have anywhere to stay; tomorrow I would probably be bitterly disappointed, but right now everything was groovy. I didn't have a care in the world.

Evening sea-bathing is one of the great pleasures in life, but the time came when I realised that even in my dream state I would not survive a night sleeping with the fishes. Clambering back into the car I decided to check out Brancaleone one more time.

There are in fact several hotels in Brancaleone, which I had failed to notice. The drive to Reggio had been completely unnecessary.

The first I came to was called the San Giorgio, and that was the one I chose.

There was something about it that drew me. When I pulled off the road I saw a grove of shady trees under which cars, an ancient lorry, a pigsty, and numerous chickens were accommodated. Unsure if this was the official car park, I drove on a few yards to an arched gate, where heavily scented jasmine grew in great profusion, almost obscuring what lay beyond.

I pushed open the gate and was greeted by a scene that has greeted me time and again since: the unique mix of people at Pensione San Giorgio. Where the family ended and the guests began it was impossible to say.

A long tiled terrace faced an abundant garden bursting with sub-tropical flowers, fruit and vegetables all jostling together: giant sunflowers towering up among ripe bursting figs, huge tomatoes festooned on groaning canes, zucchini the size of prize vegetable marrows, clouds of basilica mingling in the fragrant air with jasmine: the typical Italian kitchen garden, known as an 'ort,' taken to an extreme of horticultural art.

A genial signora in an apron advanced upon me, her grey hair framing a pink smiling face,

'Buonasera.'

The terrace was furnished with gingham-covered tables, from which a cast of characters worthy of E.M. Forster looked up and chanted, 'Buonasera!' My chef's trousers didn't seem to faze them at all.

I bowed. 'Buonasera,' I said.

The signora took me by the arm and steered me to a table. Her son Antonino stepped forward and gave me a bow, a smile, a menu, a jug of wine, a bowl of olives, a basket of bread and a bottle of sparkling mineral water, all of which were very welcome. I gestured with my hands folded beside my head to indicate sleep, and the signora said, 'Si, si, dormi qua, sicuro, non ti preoccupare.' When the feast was finished and the lamps expired there would be a bed for me tonight. I could enjoy my meal without any further effort. My work was done. Among these total strangers I felt completely at home. I picked up my menu and, pretending to read, surveyed the scene from behind it.

Two crop-haired ladies sat at one table smoking cigars, while a small child played happily among their legs. They sipped their liqueurs and blew blue smoke contentedly. They weren't actually wearing tweeds but they might as well have been, adding an air of Forsteresque sophistication to an otherwise domestic scene.

The other tables were full of Italian families, including the signora's own, descending through the generations to the grandchildren, who whizzed about on various toy conveyances, in and out and under the tables of the other diners. In the dim interior beyond, a large television blared out a game show.

Bread, olives, wine (rosso locale); maccheroni alla pastora with more wine; agnello alla griglia rosemaria alla cosentina; insalata calabrese, more wine, and for dessert, dolce di pasta frolla. After coffee I meandered upstairs to bed, my dream state considerably heightened. My 'camera' was huge, the bagno tiny, the balcone the full width of the terrace below. From it I stood beneath the stars and surveyed the dark sea beyond the pines; I could hear the waves gently murmuring. I felt a sense of peace and oneness with my surroundings. I had arrived at something pre-ordained and magical.

4

How to Buy a House

By morning word had spread. The signora brought my cappuccino and brioche to the table bursting with nervous excitement. Antonino's white shirt had obviously been ironed and pressed, so he looked like a Daz advertisement. Il Dottore Pino Tuscano would be arriving any moment to fetch me, all the way from Bova Marina.

How he knew where to find me, how they knew he was coming, how on earth anybody in this place had the faintest idea who I was or why I was there remains a mystery to this day.

When Pino arrived he was greeted with great respect. He came in through the terrace gate, not quite extending his ring to be kissed but something very like it, with all the charismatic presence of a Don.

Tall, broad, imposing, wavy-haired, forty-something, smiling genially, he was ushered to my table by the signora and her son with all possible fuss. Flecks of grey in the wavy hair, tremendous chutzpah in the manner, regal dignity in the way he extended his hand as I rose to greet him.

'Buongiorno Signor Ian.' My Calabrian godfather had arrived. Protector, consiglieri, fixer, Pino was the hub of a family system which covered the length and breadth of the Jasmine Coast.

A dentist and doctor by trade, president of the local choral society, poetry society and Amnesty International, he was in the process of running for mayor of Bova Marina. Meanwhile he had all the time in the world for me.

'Io having very small English,' he said with great deprecation.

'Don't worry,' I said, 'I have niente Italian.'

'Mia figlia Viviana will be meeting us there – she has molto buono Inglese – niente problemi di lingua oggi. Andiamo?'

I wolfed down the last of my brioche, and after being embraced by the signora and Antonino as if I were leaving home to fight in a war, I followed Pino to his car.

'Ci vediamo dopo!' my hosts called optimistically.

Conversation in the car, a Chrysler Voyager, was limited to hesitant 'sis' and 'grazies' from me, and a fullsome briefing by Pino about what to expect when we met Signor Tralongo, who, Pino explained, possibly in his capacity as a dottore, had 'a problem of physiognomy'.

'You mean he's ill?'

'Si. Malato.'

This was why he was selling, Pino was at pains to emphasise.

Under the Bridge of the White Nightingale we went, then branched immediately left along a small track I hadn't noticed before. Wild myrtle and giant cacti screened the railway track on the left, and on our right high grasses and giant eucalyptus trees sloped gently to the sea five hundred metres away. The whole place buzzed loudly with insect life. Pino's house could be seen beyond the grasses, reached by a rough track, after which, facing a ruin covered in morning glory, we came to a wall which bent sharply to the right, and there, for the first time, the full extent of what I was getting into was revealed.

Beyond a pair of imposing gates a long drive stretched, shaded by an arched tunnel of pines, towards a dilapidated terrace, which I knew surmounted the boathouse, and where much use had been made of corrugated iron and scaffolding poles. To our right a wild unkempt oleander hedge bordered an overgrown orchard, where fruit trees rioted: fig, pear, plum, apricot and pomegranate. Between the oleander and the back wall a rough track led to a garage. The place looked enormous, and well beyond my means.

We drove down the drive, turning right in front of the villa. Here a large welcoming committee was dispersed around the various features: an overgrown patch in front of the house, the boathouse to the left, the shanty-shack to the right, and running between them the low sea wall beyond which the blue Ionian twinkled. A dividing wall ran down the right-hand side, against which more corrugated iron and scaffolding leaned precariously over a white Mercedes saloon.

The occupants of the Mercedes advanced to greet me, while Celeste and the boys, plus a pretty teenage girl whom I took to be Viviana, hovered in the background until the introduction ceremony had been completed.

This is an important ritual in Italy, especially in the south; an intermediary worthy of respect by both parties effects the introductions, and continues to act as a kind of umpire from then on, to see fair play and keep the wheels of negotiation moving, with words of encouragement and advice where necessary.

Nobody could have been better suited to this task than Pino. The fact he was an old friend of Tralongo was not supposed to bias him in any way.

Signor and Senora Tralongo were small and white-haired, and Renato Tralongo had the most expressive face I've ever encountered: every emotion passed across his concertina-like wrinkles, heightening it to absurdity, like a medieval court fool. When he smiled his face lit up like a soul's awakening; when anything adverse came along it collapsed into a mask of tragic despair. My reactions to every one of the hundreds of points he proceeded to show me about his property, which he had built himself over a period of fifty years, produced these dramatic results, in a cycle as theatrical as any Mr Punch.

Working back from the garage, whose door he flung open dramatically, revealing a spacious emptiness of scuttling lizards, we made our way back through the orchard, tree by tree. The value of the place seemed to rise with every one, and my heart sank accordingly.

Tralongo was an engineer, the shanty-shack his workshop, his chief pride the well he'd sunk and the irrigation system it supplied. Pipe by pipe, tap by tap, we examined it, he and I bent over together, the rest of the party crowded around us making suggestions. I had no idea what they were talking about, but I laughed in the right places, a policy I found increasingly useful as a substitute for comprehension.

We then entered the house.

Outside it was small and undistinguished, one storey with a veranda; inside it opened up like a Tardis. Steel security shutters covered the windows, and once these were pulled up the place flooded with light. The ceiling was high and vaulted, the effect one of cool, airy space.

It was a turn-key holiday home, but it had great character; he had built it himself: two bedrooms, a bunk area, an open-plan living space with a cheap metal sink unit where a kitchen could be but wasn't. He'd built a massive ugly fireplace with an outside flue, which we all examined, Tralongo pulling out its big cork plug and puffing out his cheeks to indicate wind. It was all very ingenious.

Viviana was very friendly, very pretty, and just as fascinated by me as her brothers. She was sixteen. She was a definite distraction from the main event and she spoke enough English that we could consult and even vaguely conspire: there was no doubt she was on my side, and it was a comforting thing for a man pushing sixty in a strange land to have this Bathsheba in his corner.

Grouped finally on the boathouse terrace, which Pino explained was 'very important for sitting', we all looked out to sea. Tralongo spread his arms and breathed deeply: 'Aaaahhhh,' he said, looking at me meaningfully. The time had come.

Pino took me aside and placed his arm around my shoulders, 'You will never find…'

I knew what he meant. I would never find anywhere like this in a million years. But grave doubts still lingered: what if I couldn't afford it? What if I *could* afford it but Bunty didn't like it? Where *were* we, after all, in relation to the known world?

'Quanto costa?' I hissed, hoping for some guidance. But Pino merely shrugged his shoulders as if this was the last question on earth he could be expected to answer. He indicated Tralongo, who was watching us closely.

'Quanto?' I called, taking the bull by the horns.

He looked startled, and went into a huddle with his wife.

Apparently I was rushing my fences. Anything as final as the price probably had to be approached over a period of hours if not days, and nobody had mentioned whether it was actually for sale yet.

Nevertheless, after some considerable delay, he called out 155, 000 euros. My heart sank. 500,000 euros! It was all over.

But Viviana, standing behind Tralongo, had read my mind and divined my mistake. She held up one hand and pointed to her fingers with the other: One finger up for the hundred! Then she sketched fifty-five in the air. There had been too many 'cinque' sounding words for my bad Italian, and I was prepared for 500,000 because deep down I thought it was worth that.

My joy at the discovery that it was only 155,000 euros, a figure within my means, led me to make a classic negotiating blunder which has never been forgotten locally, passing into legend and song about the notorious gullibility of the Inglesi.

I spat on my hand like a gypsy horse trader and clapped Tralongo's in mine. I didn't try and get it down even by a penny.

He was so astonished he embraced me like a long-lost brother, his face illuminated with joy and wonder. Then everybody embraced everybody; Signora Tralongo burst into tears; Tralongo made a sad face, showing that his happiness at finding a worthy beneficiary of his life's labours was matched by his sadness at leaving this tangled paradise on its fish-teeming shore.

I looked around at the chaotic abundance – what had I done? It had all happened so fast. What on earth was I going to tell the folks at home? What if Bunty didn't like it? I had definitely committed myself now and the celebrations had already begun. Reneging on deals in southern Italy almost certainly culminates in sleeping with those teeming fish.

We repaired to a restaurant on a hillside overlooking the villa, where we could continue to admire it and toast my good fortune over a meal that lasted several hours. The jolly signora in charge, obviously an old friend, brought out dish after dish to our sunny terrace table. Whether the feast was pre-planned, or she just knew what everybody wanted, I shall never know; but like all Italian meals, especially in the south, especially if there is something to celebrate, it went on forever, until the sun was sinking low in the west. The antipasti alone were more than enough for me – at least sixteen dishes. I thought the meal was over when it hadn't even begun.

Pino ordered bottles of Vino Greca – a cut above 'Locale' – crisp and fresh and able to quickly wash away any doubts and fears I had left. Setting my sense of being on another planet aside, I entered into the spirit of the thing. After all, I told myself, as the third glass slipped soothingly down, there was no turning back.

I was hardly articulate in any language when Pino finally dropped me back at the Pensione San Giorgio. They knew immediately what must have happened and another round of embracing began. Night was falling, and Pino hugged me till I could hardly breathe, leaving me with great reluctance, and saying something complicated about 'domani', which he repeated to Antonino in case I hadn't understood.

Another feast followed, but by this time the dream state and the Vino Greca had taken over to such an extent that I can't remember anything about it, or how I got to bed in my big airy bedroom, where I woke up next morning feeling distinctly shaky.

The 'Full Consciousness Of My Position', as they call it, swiftly dawned. Bunty hadn't even seen it, yet here we were, proud owners. She didn't really even know where Calabria was. I would have to break it to her and she would have to fly down.

Pino arrived after breakfast and off we went to see architetto Napoli, in the little local town of Palizzi, under whose jurisdiction Tralongo, and now me, were bound, hand and foot I was soon to learn. In Italy the power of the local mayor and comune is pretty well absolute.

Napoli, whose function has never been entirely clear to me, wanted to see my passport, and know whether the property would be in my name, or jointly with my wife. I knew the answer to that one at least, failing to add 'if she likes it'.

He gave me a map of the place and told me, after much interpreting, that if I would sign an agreement to buy it in three months' time, he would by then hope to have all the documenti in order, which Tralongo had mistakenly thought were, but in fact were not.

This was a get-out, of course. There was definite nervousness in the room, and they wanted me to sign there and then. But even here in Byzantine Calabria, under Napoleonic or any other law, such an agreement couldn't possibly be binding. I could simply fly away, and Tralongo could sell to someone else if he got a better offer. There wouldn't, in practical terms, be anything either of us could do about it.

'He will be happy to hand over the keys to you now.'

Clearly he didn't expect to get a better offer, and anyway I didn't want to get out of it. What was I to do? The obvious thing would be to say that Bunty needed to fly down and take a look at it first, but if the sale became contingent on that, I would be guilty of a breach of the honour code whereby yesterday we had celebrated. I didn't want to spoil the carnival atmosphere, or the sense of it being the most exciting thing that had happened here for years, and of being accepted into the midst of these strange, delightful people. Equally, I didn't want to be swindled in some subtle and cunning way, which at the moment I couldn't quite figure out. It came down to this: could I or could I not trust them, and put my faith in Pino's good will? It was a question of 'Buon Fidele'.

I thought about it. The idea that Celeste and her children could possibly be mixed up in anything underhand was out of the question. I had stumbled onto their beach under the undoubted auspices of Destino, and the fact there was something for sale in that tiny place only emphasised it. I had thought the price a steal just as Tralongo obviously had: it was a good deal for both of us. That number of euros in those far-off days came to £87,000. As Pino said, you will never find: you will never find two acres of sub-tropical paradise with a hundred-metre frontage onto an all-but-private beach on any other Mediterranean coast in Europe. The place was unique. But was it too good to be true?

As it turned out, whatever they wanted me to sign needed by

law to be translated, so I had to get Bunty down there before that happened.

For the sake of form I said, 'But what if the documents *aren't* ready in three months?'

This produced gales of laughter and one of the greatest displays of shrugging I had yet seen. It also produced a word I was to hear many times again.

The word was 'Speriamo'.

Speriamo means a lot more than just 'Let's hope so'. It signifies a whole philosophy of life. In an uncertain world, future events, good or bad, may or may not happen. There's no point thinking about them or worrying or trying to predict them. To the Calabrese mind the only course that makes any sense is to shrug and say 'Speriamo'.

It doesn't exactly express indifference, though it can, to the uninitiated outsider, seem like it. It isn't that they don't take things seriously – though with most northern European preoccupations they don't. They just have worked out, quite correctly, that you can't change fate, so you might as well not bother to try, and in the meantime do your absolute best to enjoy yourself.

'Caffè?' The eternal question. So we repaired to a bar and had some delicious espresso.

Pino dropped me back, so at last I could retrieve my car and find a phone box where no one would overhear me.

'Mama? Is that you?' I call her Mama (she is in fact one quarter Italian).

'About *time*! Where *are* you?'

'In Calabria, I told you.'

'What's it like?'

'You would not believe, honestly.'

'Believe what? What've you done?'

'How do you mean, *done*?'

'You haven't done something silly with the money?'

In explaining how things stood, I knew that diplomacy was needed, as it probably would be with any wife.

'I haven't done anything silly and not a penny has changed hands.'

'But why *would* it change hands?'

'Well I *have* found something, if you must know. You have to come and see it.'

'But I can't come *now*!'

'You have to.'

Reggio airport is, or was then, even smaller than Brindisi or Palma in the fifties. In Palma there had been Franco's Guardia Civil, armed to the teeth; here there were military carabinieri in battle fatigues toting automatic weapons

Bunty came wandering through, looking a bit shell-shocked, her hair in a frizz. All she could think about was those weapons. As luck would have it, they were transporting an important mafia prisoner on her plane.

'Are those soldiers waiting for the mafia guy? He was on my *plane*.'

It wasn't a good start.

In the car I said, 'All that stuff about the mafia is greatly exaggerated,' trying to disentangle us from the airport perimeter and get on the coast highway.

'I was told we'd be crazy to come down here – they said it was bandit country.'

'Bandit country! Who said that?'

'I can't remember. Someone.'

'What utter nonsense people talk!'

'How do you know it's nonsense?'

'How do you know it isn't?'

'I don't. I just think if everybody says something it might be true, that's all.'

'Nobody knows anything about Calabria. They don't even know where it is.'

'You got that right.'

We buzzed along the SS 106 until at last the worst of the dereliction and half-finished buildings began to diminish, and olive and lemon groves started to appear. The sun was shining on the sea, and I reflected that hope springs eternal.

'We're coming to the Jasmine Coast quite soon,' I said. 'It's really beautiful.'

The traffic was light as usual, mainly ancient Fiat Pandas going incredibly slowly, or new Fiat Puntos going incredibly fast. Suddenly a black Porsche SUV with blacked-out windows flew past us.

'There you are!' Bunty said. 'What did I tell you?'

'How d'you mean – *there you are!*'

'You know – who else would be driving a car like that?'

'You're not still on about the mafia?'

'Who else did you think that was?'

There was no point arguing. People are always going to believe what they want to believe. And anyway I couldn't deny the existence of the 'Ndrangheta. I just didn't think they would be all that interested in us. Whether or not the people I'd met so far were 'connected' I couldn't honestly say. Certainly things down here seemed highly irregular.

By the time we got to Spropoli I'd pointed out as many beautiful features as I could, but she still seemed unconvinced. I think it's got a lot to do with individual expectations. In my case, I saw what I wanted to see, and it was the same with her. I wanted her to see the beautiful sea, but she seemed fixated on shabby buildings and black cars.

When we turned onto my famous waste ground, the two communal rubbish bins seemed painfully apparent. Under the Bridge of the White Nightingale someone had dumped their fridge.

The rough track seemed rougher than before, and a train hurtled by.

'That's the Seaside Line,' I said, hopefully.

'Doesn't it have a fence?'

'No.'

At the gate I had keys, but none of them fitted. We stared down the unkempt drive.

'It's certainly jolly big!' she said.

I wasn't sure if this was a plus or a minus. I said, 'It's right on the beach.'

'How come you've got those keys?'

'Oh, I've met the owner and he just gave them to me.'

It didn't sound plausible, unless there was a lot more to it than that, which of course there was.

'Why on earth would he do that?'

I decided that further prevarication was pointless.

'If you must know I've sort of said we'll buy it – unless you really don't like it. I just thought it seemed such a bargain. Wait till you see it – it really is right on this amazing beach.'

'How much?'

'At first I thought he said five hundred thousand – I honestly thought it was worth that – but then it turned out he'd said only a hundred and fifty-five thousand euros.'

I waited with bated breath.

'How much is that in pounds?'

'Eighty-seven thousand.'

'Hmm. It is jolly big.' And she started climbing over the gate.

I followed her down the drive as she headed for the sea. When she reached the beach she stopped and looked around.

'It's incredible.'

'Too good to miss, I thought. I mean, you weren't here and it all sort of escalated.'

'This beach is amazing.'

'So you think I did the right thing?'

'I don't know how you could possibly have found it.'

'No, nor do I.'

'What happens now?'

'That's a good question. They want us to sign a weird document.'

'Oh, God.'

I explained as best I could how things stood. 'When it's translated we might get a better idea. We have to go to the notario in Bova Marina to sign it.'

'Shouldn't we get a lawyer?'

'I suppose we should, but I haven't the first idea how we'd find one in a place like this.'

At the appointed hour we went to Bova Marina and got lost. I was just giving up when I spotted Tralongo's car looking for us. Signora Tralongo was in tears, but I reassured her and introduced her to Bunty.

At the notario's office a large number of people had gathered, presided over by the 'dottoressa', an imposing lady in black to whom all deferred. The documents were spread upon her desk, in English and Italian. Bunty and I went into a huddle; Signora Tralongo started crying again, and was comforted by Pino. Pino made a big impression on Bunty; she was quite certain he was a mafia godfather.

'Well at least he's *our* godfather,' I muttered, not wishing such a word to be overheard.

The document said we'd buy the place in three months' time for the agreed price, during which period Tralongo wouldn't sell to anyone else. I would return in January with the money. If the documents weren't ready by then the deal was off. It all seemed pretty straightforward.

The witnesses were at the ready, the dottoressa poised with her enormous stamp. The many bystanders held their breath. I said to Pino, 'Don't you think we ought to have a lawyer?'

'You must have confidence in me,' he said.

A sigh of relief filled the room as we meekly signed; at least Bunty was in it with me now. We both still harboured the gravest doubts, and these were only heightened when Pino took us to one side in a conspiratorial manner.

'Signor Tralongo has one small favour to ask,' he said.

'Oh, yes?'

'It is the custom here that part of the price is paid in cash. He would like you to do this.'

'How much of it?'

'A hundred thousand euros.'

'What! But that's almost all of it!'

Pino spread his hands in the most deprecating manner.

'It is the custom.'

'I don't how I can get that much cash.'

'It is the only payment he is able to receive.' I could see Signora Tralongo weeping gently in the background. I said I supposed so if only to cheer her up. My own wife didn't look too happy either.

Back at Pino's house a feast of pasticcini had been prepared and a lethal liquor called limoncello to toast the deal. Tralongo sat gloomily at the table, his face a tragic mask.

'The Inglese has bought my house, yet I have no money.'

Viaggio con il Diavolo

It isn't as easy as you might think to go into your bank and draw out 100,000 euros in cash, even if you have it in your account. Suspicions are immediately raised, and you have to explain why you want it.

'But it's *my* money!'

Explaining about Signor Tralongo's preferences and the customs of Calabria was obviously out of the question. I started to feel like a criminal myself, at the very least a party to some tax scam I didn't understand, if not a drug deal.

It took the best part of my three months to persuade them that I hadn't taken up cocaine smuggling, and for them to reluctantly assemble the euros and even more reluctantly hand them over.

'We still strongly advise an electronic transfer,' was their final word, as they pushed the surprisingly slim packets through the window. They provided a security guard to escort me to my car.

It just goes to show how electronic we've become – the last thing anyone expects you to pay with is cash.

My daughter Mia bought me a flesh-coloured money belt, and this we proceeded to stuff. We packed my Renault Clio to the rafters with everything we thought I might need for a lengthy stay in a house with no furniture.

At last the moment came and the whole family assembled in our street to see me off. We hugged and laughed and made the kind of jokes people make when loved ones leave for war zones. My sense of unreality, and the unspoken thought that they might never see me again, preyed on my mind as I headed for the Channel Tunnel train.

Once in France the thing I hadn't thought of became quickly apparent: don't attempt to cross the Massif Central in January; the whole place freezes up.

The blizzards began early, just after dark on Day One, as I headed south on the A26 to Rheims. What with everything but the kitchen sink on board, I hadn't been able to see much in the first place. Add a few lorryloads of slush, old overloaded wipers, frozen washers, huge snowflakes lit by blazing headlights, a road surface rapidly becoming a frozen bog, the whole nightmare being played out at a crazy speed from which it was impossible to slow down because of pressure from behind, you had a recipe for someone needing to get off the motorway urgently.

I got off at the next exit, and paid at the caisse, at that hour still thankfully manned. I asked the guy about a hotel, but couldn't quite catch what he said – something about douze kilomètres.

But in what direction? Once clear of the lit autoroute, all became darkest night over white whiteout. Not even the road could be seen in that sea of white: I was soon lost, with the mounting realisation that I wouldn't last long out here. The petrol would run out and with it life-giving warmth; instead of death on the highway it looked like death from exposure and hypothermia. There was no sign of anything but glimmering, sinister white.

At times like these something superhuman kicks in; some instinct for survival. Either that or it doesn't, and you die. In my case I realised that, as my eyes got used to the white-tinted dark, I could just make out a faint glow on the horizon; the lights of the very caisse I'd so recently passed through.

How long it took to get back I'll never know – it seemed forever; I had to keep getting out to chart a path free of fatal obstacles; one false move would have meant the end.

The terror and confusion of the motorway came as a relief the second time around – something almost to be revelled in. I entered it with a new desperate determination – a kind of madness.

Rheims came at last, and with it the hope of a hotel. I could see neon signs for several in the distance, from the vantage point of a raised section of road. But how I could reach them I had no idea. I've still no idea, and I've never found them again, even on a sunny afternoon.

But on that dreadful night, by keeping them in view come what may, I was gradually drawn into their orbit and found myself in a quadrangle of motorway hotels packed together, but not as packed as the milling mob of cars and travellers seeking shelter from that unforgiving nightmare.

And they all spoke French – were French. Even after passing what I thought was the winning post, the reward of a bed remained a mirage: concierge after concierge turned me away.

At last I got the last bed in the last hotel, an unoccupied chambre de domestique, little more than a cupboard. I said, 'Vous avez sauvez ma vie!'

In the morning the general idea was that we were here for the duration: all roads out were impassable. I munched on a croissant and decided to ignore them, joining a small convoy of other intrepid souls headed south.

Once back on the motorway people were dropping like flies, but somehow I kept going. My wipers and windscreen washers were frozen solid and I nearly missed the Lyons turn-off because it was covered in snow. No effort was being made by the gendarmes to clear things up.

The route gradually rises until the apex of the Massif is reached and the long descent into the Saône Valley begins. I knew if I could only reach those golden Burgundy slopes my ordeal would be over. 'O for a beaker full of the warm South' about summed it up.

But it's a long way up and many didn't make it. They littered the roadside in disconsolate groups, blowing on their hands and talking into their phones. As often as not the casualties were cars far larger and more modern than mine, but somehow the overloaded Clio kept going.

The next problem was petrol; most fillings stations were frozen over and closed, but along with pretty well every other survivor on that hellish road I found the only open one. The tailback from the pumps seemed interminable, and it was touch and go whether I would reach them before they or I ran out of fuel. The anxiety was a hazard in itself.

It was mid-afternoon by the time I finally filled my tank with every last drop I could squeeze in, and had a paper cup of espresso from a machine. It was the turning point: I didn't know it but my ordeal was almost over; a few kilometres further and the autoroute merged with the A5, which sloped south in long majestic curves through green countryside, into the Saône Valley and the glorious vineyards of Burgundy.

I stopped before Lyons, shattered, in a hotel set back from a filling station. My headache had become a migraine, and I lay on the tiled floor of my surprisingly grand bathroom throwing up feebly into the toilette. After a while I mustered the strength to crawl into bed.

In the morning I was ravenously hungry and took advantage of a cunning device the French have perfected for boiling eggs in large numbers in a sort of basket thing: you load it up, lower it into the boiling water, and when the thing goes ping you're in business.

Half a dozen of these, several croissants later, washed down by a gallon or so of coffee, and I left that hotel a new man.

It's a lucky thing I was, because the next challenge was just as daunting as the last: the seven circles of hell that is the Lyons gyratory system.

Green signs and blue, the confusion grew, as I struggled to reach the road for Chambéry-Torino. But try as I might, slowly but surely, I was inexorably sucked, like some helpless pond creature in a whirlpool, into the unforgiving heart of Lyons Centre.

For some time it seemed I would never get out again and was doomed to spend the rest of my life in Lyons. Toll after toll, often involving throwing coins into a basket, nearly always the wrong ones, took me round and round in circles, until I was sure I'd been through most of them at least twice.

In the end, more by luck than judgement, and taking into account the law of averages, my number came up and the word 'Chambéry' appeared on a blue sign above the lane in which I found myself. It took several heart-stopping kilometres for me to believe I was at last clear of Lyons.

Up and up into the Alps I went, through the Fréjus tunnel – as long and scary as a ghost train in hell for the claustrophobe – and then at last I was in Italy.

Italy! Oh the joy of it! I stopped at the very next service station. A cappuccino, a double freshly squeezed blood orange and a panini hot from the griddle – it was all so wondefully different from France. On the uphill Alpine haul it had drizzled depressingly on sad-looking clusters of Swiss-looking chalets. Here the sun shone on towering peaks topped by Norman castles impossibly perched over green valleys. The pretty Italian girls serving in the Autogrill laughed and gossiped.

'Italia!' I beamed. 'Molto bravo!'

'Inglese?'

'Si, Inglese.'

'Sempre piove là, si?'

'Si, si,' I guffawed disloyally, 'sempre piove in Inghilterra.'

Barstanders joined in the general salutations and raised their glasses to the fact that in England it always rained, whereas here in Italy it was 'sempre sole!'

I headed for the A10 at Genoa, the first available road on the Mediterranean coast to Rome. Genoa appears suddenly. One minute you're in a succession of mountain tunnels, the next you're pitched into the midst of yellow palaces facing bright blue sea. The effect is dramatic, as is the fast, winding road along the Ligurian Riviera.

It started to rain, gently at first, then hard, then torrentially. It got pitch dark and the road became a river: one minute I was heading for Rome on the Aurelian Way, thinking about the Emperor Tiberius, next I was driving through a waterfall.

I turned off blind. I didn't have time to think, just turned onto what looked like a side road. It plunged straight down into a river.

Next thing I knew the car was filling with water and I was sinking fast. Clutching my money belt, I clambered out and scrambled up the bank.

The darkness was impenetrable; the only sound the relentless drumming of the rain. I was back in the middle of nowhere, only this time it looked terminal. My great adventure was over.

I stood there in the rain for a while, letting it wash over me, waiting for an idea, or for something to happen, perhaps a miracle. Nothing happened, so I did the only thing I could: I got back into that river and pushed.

The car was still far enough above the surface that I could get some purchase through the open driver's window and gradually the thing began to move, first towards, then partially up, the opposite bank. Once the engine was clear of the water I opened the bonnet and wedged my umbrella, useless to me now in my half-drowned state, in a protective shield over the drenched machinery. I don't know much about engines, but I knew this one needed to get dry. Then I removed the keys and set off to seek help.

I didn't have much hope and I thought the chances of the car recovering were zero, but I headed back to the Aurelian Way because I thought I'd glimpsed a house just before disaster struck.

Sure enough, on the other side of the wide, deserted highway, something white glimmered through a dense cluster of pines.

The house was in darkness, but I knocked anyway. After a while a light came on and suddenly I was surrounded by a large family of Italians, who'd all got out of bed. An old man sat me down in front of a television to watch a football match between Juventus and Real Madrid, while the next generation prepared a meal and argued volubly over whether some form of rescue service might be reached before morning. The youngest generation stared at me round-eyed: an alien being who'd given them the gift of a midnight adventure.

When I'd eaten enough spaghetti to sink a battleship it was announced that an SOS truck would meet me at the car. At least that's what I thought they said, based on what they thought I'd said.

After an emotional farewell I made my way back to the dismal scene at the river. I wasn't convinced that anyone could possibly know where it was, but at least it had stopped raining.

The silence and darkness were as impenetrable as ever and after a while I climbed into the car, more as a means of sitting down than anything else. Idly I turned the key in the ignition. The chances of it starting were nil, but it started. Unbelievably, that sunken lifeless thing was transformed into a vehicle once more; a vehicle that leapt up the opposite riverbank and flew off into the night like a scalded cat.

I didn't know where we were going, but at least we were going. And I wasn't turning back into that river, so I continued along a gravel lane that wound its way through olive groves, until it came out into a small cluster of houses. And on the side of one of them was the magic word 'Albergo'.

I watched late-night Italian television in my room until the flickering images and incomprehensible story brought peace to my quivering nervous system, and sleep, which Shakespeare says 'knits up the raveled sleave of care', stole over me at last.

In the morning the welcoming padrone, who had not minded my unexpected late-night check-in, set about getting me off to a good start.

He sizzled lots of bacon and eggs, possibly because I was English, with rounds of salami picante thrown in for good measure. Large fresh brown brioches with warm yellow centres were piled up to make Italian-style butties; cappuccino followed cappuccino, and for the second day running I was boosted on my way with enough calories and caffeine and sugar to carry me over whatever further hurdles lay in store.

These were, apart from the pump attendant at Naples trying to sell me an oil-change and a puppy, concentrated in the mountainous unpredictable Autostrada del Sole, the misleadingly upbeat name they give the A3.

Here my final catastrophe occurred, at Reggio, just when I

thought I'd made it. I missed the sharp right onto the SS 106, carrying straight on along a backstreet which moments before had been an autostrada.

Reggio is a place where it's easy to get lost and almost impossible to escape, especially if you're dog-tired. I pulled into a service station and gave up.

So near and yet so far, I waited for something to happen. After a while two students arrived on a Vespa, one of whom spoke English. The girl had an aunt who lived in Spropoli, 'Bellissima'.

They led me back to the 106 and waved goodbye, me calling 'come and see me on my beach!'

They never did – I wish they would! They saved my life that evening.

Meanwhile I'd had all I could take of that interminable journey, and drove from then on at a risk-free snail's pace until the familiar sign of the Pensione San Giorgio hove into view.

6

How to Build a House

We reassembled in the dottoressa's office in far greater numbers than before. Witnesses from both sides filled the room, mainly female relations, in my case Pino and Celeste's.

A girl called Giuliana was there, retained by Renato Tralongo as an interpreter, and when the dottoressa read the contract she decided it should be translated for me word for word, in private, so she could be sure I understood everything.

Giuliana would explain it all as we went along, and this meant removing me forthwith to her mother's house in Reggio, where her computer was. We would reconvene tomorrow.

A great furore ensued, with much weeping from Signora Tralongo and lamentations from witnesses, but the dottoressa's word was final.

I climbed into Giuliana's car, conscious of the tightness of my money belt, which I really had been hoping to shed. Every day you wander about packing that much cash is tempting providence further.

Giuliana enjoyed the drama, and the upset to the Tralongos, whom she heartily disliked and who would now have to pay her extra. Her one dream was to live in London, and having me as an unexpected friend was an added bonus. All the way to Reggio she pumped me for details. Having someone to talk to in English made explaining how London functioned, and where I lived, and that London isn't one place but many, a relaxing way of passing the time.

She was a serious girl, married to a policeman in Sicily, whose job with the Banditry Suppression Taskforce was very dangerous.

'Is that the anti-mafia?' I asked.

'Sshh, we don't say that word.'

The only thing she couldn't understand was why a 'person like me' would want to come here when I lived in the world's most desirable place.

'For you, yes, but I was born in London. Here is so different – so unspoilt.'

'Not unspoilt – abbandonato!'

Her mother lavished cakes and coffee on us while we laboured through the contract, keeping a discreet distance and yet a hawk-like eye on her daughter, alone in the room with a strange man. You could tell she thought it all very unconventional and shocking.

We discovered that Renato Tralongo, 'a single man' had 'built it with his own hand'.

'A single man?' I asked.

'He is not even married to that woman.'

We thought this a fascinating discovery.

Next day the atmosphere was more charged than ever as the dottoressa turned page after page. Finally she rose and seated herself at an enormous machine, a bit like an organ, whose ivory keys she struck with great deliberation. Slowly but surely, clunk, clunk, clunk, my purchase of Signor Tralongo's property was enshrined in law.

'You may give him the money now,' the dottoressa said to me in English, and a great sigh rippled through the room.

I undid my shirt, but the money belt was stuck under my waistband. I undid my trousers and they fell down.

Comedy plus relief equals uproar. The women screamed with laughter and clutched themselves, sat down or simply fell over. Even the dottoressa smiled. Then all the money spilled out on the floor. There was pandemonium as different parties claimed the right to gather it and count it. The place was a bedlam of scrambling women and scattered banknotes.

At last it lay in orderly bundles on the dottoressa's table and Tralongo admitted gloomily it was all there. The house was mine. I was hugged and congratulated and kissed until my head spun. It only remained to cross the road to the bank and transfer the small legitimate bit.

At last alone, I drove slowly back to what I could now call home. I felt dazed. The road winds along the coast from the headland of the Madonna of the Ships at Bova Marina, past bays and beaches, pines and palms – was this not paradise?

I certainly hoped so, but those nagging doubts still lingered. You hear so many stories of people being fleeced in foreign lands. Were this morning's proceedings really legal? Was the house really mine, with all that land? Surely that impressive dottoressa couldn't be a party to some scam.

I'd been heading for the San Giorgio, but decided instead to go to the house. I'd never really been there on my own, 'in possession'; never really thought of it as mine. I wanted to occupy it, get to know every stick of it. I needed to live in it, inhabit it, stop being a visitor staying in a hotel like a tourist.

It wasn't easy. Tiled floors and no furniture don't make for comfort on cold nights, and the January nights were chilly under the stars. Grey storms blew in, bending the trees, driving the rain and the huge waves that came right up over the sea wall.

Not having a bed was the worst part. Tralongo had left some small, single, sagging ones, but I longed for something big and comfortable. There was no kitchen in the house, and I cooked on an ancient gas stove in the barakka powered by a gas 'bombola'.

And there was no television. It gets awfully lonely on your own without a television.

The whole family was coming for a holiday in the summer and the plan was that I would get the place ready by then. This entailed creating more leibensraum by converting the boathouse into a house. We shipped 50,000 euros down into my new bank account, which we thought should cover everything. How wrong we were!

The building project, which to Bunty and I seemed a simple one, meant my first introduction to 'The Family System'.

Put simply, rather than wasting time seeking competitive estimates and alternative suppliers, and letting the marketplace decide, someone will always have a cousin.

Gianni is Celeste's cousin as well as Pasquale's. He lives with his family in a large house across the main road from mine, and he also owns a strip of land one plot along from me, his 'ort', where he grows vegetables and fruit in great abundance. He parks his fishing boat there, which can be slipped easily into the sea, just like mine could from my boathouse if I had one, which I don't, nor am I ever likely to if Bunty has anything to do with it.

The garden of his house, where his ancient father still presides, is a veritable farm, stretching up the hillside behind. Here chickens and a pig augment the family diet, plus Gianni makes wine from his vineyard somewhere in the mountains.

In a nutshell, his is precisely the way of life I'd been searching for.

Pino and Celeste introduced him the very next day after the purchase.

There was no arrangement or warning. One minute I was sitting serenely, ruler of all I surveyed, staring out to sea, thinking how nice it was to be alone at last and not to have to struggle with Italian and pretend to understand what was going on. Next the air was full of car noise and Calabrese. They just came down the drive and arrived.

I was neither expecting nor ready for them, and this was to be the pattern to this day. You never know who or what is going to happen to you next.

I leapt up and willed myself into buongiorno mode, not always easy, one main obstacle being the dress code. As usual I was wearing something far below Pino's sartorial standard, and Gianni was dressed to the nines for the occasion: blue shirt, pressed trousers, smart shoes – he looked thoroughly uncomfortable, much like Joe Gargery when he comes up to London to visit 'Mister' Pip. His face glowed with an obviously recent shave, his shock of dark hair wouldn't lie down, and he clenched and unclenched his hands as if they couldn't wait to grip onto something manual. He held one of them out to me, and when the introductions were complete he kissed me on both cheeks, muttering, 'Bravo, bravo.'

'Gianni will be your Capo di Operai – he will arrange everything,' Pino announced. 'He is Celeste's cousin.'

Gianni smiled the stubborn smile I was to come to know so well.

'But we don't know what we're doing yet!' I said, using our usual mix of signs and odd words from either language, Gianni nodding sagely throughout.

'Architetto Napoli is preparing a skitch.'

The skitch arrived the next day, along with Napoli, his assistant, Pino, Celeste, Gianni and various other people. There seemed to be a swimming pool and several other things I'd never mentioned. In fact I'd never mentioned anything and the whole project came as a complete surprise. Bunty had said something about 'a little cottage'. The skitch looked more like a burgeoning palazzo.

When I mentioned this to Pino, he simply shrugged and said, 'It is only a skitch.'

The following morning I was woken by the deafening racket of Gianni's trattore clanking down the drive. It was barely seven a.m.

He looked much happier in his working clothes and greeted me gaily, 'Ciao Ian.'

'Buongiorno Gianni!'

'Per lavoro.'

'Caffè, Gianni?'

'No, grazie, no.'

'I'm going to have to have some.'

'Si, si.' He waved me back into doing whatever I was talking about, a matter of total indifference to him. When I came out again, shaved and carrying my cafetière (a completely alien instrument to any self-respecting Italian), he was smashing down the whole boat-house terrace structure by bulldozing it with his tractor and then finishing it off with a sledgehammer.

This would be an alarming thing for any householder. I hadn't said he should do it, had no idea it was his plan. On the other hand it was too late now and I didn't know how to say whatever it was I wanted to say.

Which was what? In order to build whatever it was we were building, perhaps it was necessary to raze everything to the ground first.

I was just about to say something, when down the drive came a lorry with a mechanical digger on the back, driven by Nino, the second member of our team.

Nino was burly and taciturn, very much the proud Calabrese. His truck and digger give him a certain status and he climbed down from the cab like a conquistador.

Gianni introduced me, but my mind was on that digger. What on earth was going to happen now?

I pointed to it and made various other agitated gestures.

'Tranquillo, Ian!' said Gianni. 'Non ti preoccupare.' This is what they said to me, and they're still saying it.

We were going to dig a hole behind the boathouse, now flattened like a Roman ruin, to enlarge the foundations for the building proposed in architetto Napoli's skitch. This Gianni explained with great patience, so that in the end I understood. His method of teaching me Italian, which he eventually did after a fashion, was to repeat words over and over, with hand gestures and other theatrics, some extremely inventive, until finally I got it. Stubbornness was the key to Gianni's methods and his nature.

As soon as I got the general idea I joined in the debate about the dimensions of the hole. There was a beautiful old olive tree, which they were about to tear out, and this became my first of many battlegrounds with them.

'No!' I said, grasping the trunk and shaking my head.

They didn't give in easily and I didn't trust them even then not to accidentally wreck its root system. But the olive tree stands to this day, shading the entrance to the 'casa di barce', defining its western limit; an important marker in many ways.

This was the first step in the abandonment of the skitch.

Once I realised that anything was possible and that we were

digging my own 'Calabria Suite', I wanted it to be as big as possible. Allowing for the olive tree, there was no other reason I, or they, could see not to maximise. The skitch version looked too small. Given free choice and all this land, who wouldn't want a grand bedroom and bathroom? Bunty's 'little cottage' also went by the board at this point.

I felt a terrifying sense of power and recklessness once that digger went to work. The earth piled up, the hole grew and blind faith in total strangers whose language I couldn't speak was all I had to go on. But the intoxication of building a dwelling place, of creating something out of nothing, awoke some primitive instinct deep within me.

At ten o'clock they downed tools and Gianni, with stubborn patience, finally got it through to me that my job was to go and get the paninis.

I sallied forth into Galati and found a small shop which sold them, along with groceries of all kinds. A girl stood behind the glass deli counter being ordered about by a tiny old woman at the till. Several people were waiting, either to be served, or for her to add up their bill, or for no apparent reason other than passing the time of day.

The tiny old tartar was not to be rushed, and totted up the totals with agonising deliberation, each item entered in the till and then repeated out loud – vente-tre, quaranta-due, cinquanta-quatro – the numbers droning on like a mantra, filling the air with a kind of miasma of slowness.

Nobody except me, of course, with my inbred notions of urgency and anxiety imported from the big city, was in the least bit put out by this – it was the pace of life they were used to. Their minds and bodies operated normally at this speed. The idea of being 'kept waiting' – with the single exception of driving – is virtually unknown. Once someone's bill was finally calculated the padronessa would enquire about their health, family and any other gossip that applied, much of which could be joined in with by the other shoppers; all save me.

'Salve, bon giorno.' At last it was my turn.

I had to give my order to the tiny woman, who then passed it on to the girl. Any attempt to short-circuit this system was ruthlessly suppressed. The idea that the two of them might serve two customers at once was anathema.

Naturally everyone was interested to know what the Inglese was going to order. None of them had seen an Inglese before. They all knew who I was of course, and where I lived, and everything about me, so they listened intently to my every word.

'Due panini, per favore – no, tre.' I thought I'd have one too.

'Come?' The tiny woman didn't seem to get it, so I turned to the girl and repeated myself. She looked extremely alarmed and repeated it back to the tiny woman, who repeated it back to her before turning back to me and saying, 'Prosciutto? Formaggio? Salami?' The girl leaned forward in readiness, as did everyone else.

Gianni hadn't said, or if he had I'd forgotten, so I went for one of each, but that wasn't the end of it. Prosciutto crudo or cotto, salami piccante or dolce, any number of cheeses; it was a relief when finally the girl got to work, a decision having been reached by a democratic process involving everyone in the shop.

I bought beer and Coke and, the interminable billing process finally complete, departed to a chorus of arrivedercis. The Inglese had definitely arrived.

Next day Nino brought a big yellow cement mixer, an object that has hardly left the premises since. The Romans invented cement and nothing ever really happens in Italy until tons of it have been poured.

Nino isn't a cousin, but Gianni does have a cousin called Nino, and he too arrived that morning for the first of many times. Nino di Palizzi (as opposed to Brancaleone where the first Nino comes from) provides building supplies, and his lorry rattled down the drive laden with them.

There was some rusty-looking steel mesh (rete di ferro) for laying in the hole preparatory to cementing, sacks of cement and a big pile of sand.

Nino was ruddy-faced and affable, and handed me a bill. As he shook hands he looked up at the sky with a satisfied smile. 'Sempre sole!' he said.

I hurried into the house to get the money, but when I returned he laughed.

'No, no, non è necessario adesso – più tardi – come in Africa!'

When he left Gianni grinned at me and said, 'Sempre soldi [always money].'

I didn't get the joke right away, but I soon did. Before long Nino was known simply as 'Nino sempre soldi'.

Soon the mixer was churning and I was off again to get paninis. When I got back the foundations were laid out in a glistening wet apron. Things were proceeding apace.

Next day the cement lorry arrived, and this is when I first met the indispensible Pasquale. Silver-haired and silver-tongued, the third and most important of Gianni's cousins, in his sunglasses and crisp white shirt he seemed more like a film director than an 'operaio'. Having been introduced to me he surveyed the scene with a critical eye, before turning to direct operations with the cement lorry.

I thought we'd poured our own cement, but I was wrong. What we had done was merely prepare for something far more massive. The cement lorry, a familiar sight in Italy, looks like a giant pink-and-green striped ice cream gently revolving as it drives along. When it stops and is ready for action, the revolutions increase and the cement comes surging down a giant tube. It took all the combined strength of Gianni, Nino and Pasquale to control the lashing machinations of this tube, while the driver controlled the flow. Gradually they hauled the nozzle to and fro, until the hole was filled to the brim, nearly a foot deep. Our maverick building plan was literally set in stone; nothing short of a nuclear bomb could change it now.

After the driver had exchanged the usual pleasantries with every-one the lorry roared off up the drive, ripping branches off my trees as it went.

Next day Nino di Palizzi was back, laden with grey breeze-blocks, and the walls started to go up. We weren't sure where the windows and doors went and by now the skitch was completely obsolete, so I set about designing my ideal beachside bedroom: plenty of light, I thought, and bella vistas.

Soon after this architetto Napoli paid us a surprise site visit and didn't seem too happy. He went off in a huff, returning the next day with Pino. It was a bit like being reported to the headmaster.

Architetto Napoli's skitch looked like a child's drawing, the sort of thing you see pinned to walls in primary schools. His real function went far beyond mere architecture, deep into the Byzantine heart of that most untransparent and alarming body, the Comune di Palizzi.

Alarming to me, at least, because, like so many other things, I didn't understand it. Fear of the unknown joined forces with my deep-rooted fear of authority.

Whether or not they had passed this skitch, or given it the nod, or even seen it, I never knew. But the fact it had been contravened, and so cavalierly, was likely to do me harm, Pino explained. Architetto Napoli was not a person it was wise to upset.

In addition, Gianni was a party to it, and Gianni and Napoli were engaged in some sort of long-running feud.

Having made their point they made a critical tour of my fledgling house, finally dubbing it the 'Casa di Troppe Finestre' – far too many windows, they said, and all far too big.

This had the effect of bonding me and my co-conspirators closer – 'Contra Mundum'. We didn't want any more site visits, and a childish tendency to demonise architetto Napoli took root among us.

This of course suited Gianni, who was already at war with him – I never knew why. And Gianni liked to be in charge of things, a tendency he shared with Pasquale. Nino only wanted to get on with it, rarely offering anything other than a wry smile and a headshake.

I had a big thick picture book called *Seaside Style* which Bunty had given me, and the more I showed it to them the wryer Nino's smile became. In particular I'd found a house in the Aeolian Islands that I wanted mine to end up looking like. It had a beautiful blue terrace, surrounded by seating made to look like white, rolling waves, with flower beds set behind low, blue-topped walls, and a generally 'distressed' appearance. The fact it belonged to an Italian, which I'd hoped might help them relate, failed to do so.

And so we soldiered on, they with their fixed ideas, me with mine, and very little common ground between us. The cultural divide was exacerbated by the problema di lingua, which they were able to hide behind, three against one. Whenever they wanted to disagree they simply pretended not to understand.

'Non si capisce!!!' And three synchronised shrugs.

7

The Family System

Behind the wall to the right of the property lay a low bungalow almost totally hidden from view, on a strip of land the same length as ours but narrower. This was the domain of the 'professore'.

Bunty and I had peered over his wall and decided that he looked like an ideal neighbour; bits and pieces of funky stuff lay around his garden: a couple of old boats, and, in particular, a caravan. Bunty took a great fancy to this caravan. It seemed to speak of sixties hippies and the alternative lifestyle of our hazily remembered youth. We had somehow got it into our heads that he was a professor of classical antiquities.

The area inside our gates, behind the orchard, was a dead zone, and here, instead of wasteland, why not put a caravan of our own? This is what Bunty thought and it was up to me to find one. With our large family and friends, almost any number of bedrooms would never be enough, and they were all arriving in August, a mere six months away.

One day, having looked up the word for caravan I explained the idea to Gianni.

But he of course had a better one, and next day appeared with a large, colourful newspaper advertisement for a 'Casa di Legno'. He was extremely excited and as far as I could gather, a 'collega' of his had something to do with it. All it meant was for me to drive up into the mountains, to Serra San Bruno.

We all gathered round the picture and the democratic process took its course. Nino shook his head and smiled wryly, but Pasquale was in favour. That left me.

It seemed churlish to refuse to even investigate, and Gianni managed to convince me that a caravan would cost the same if not more. The wooden house was 'molto più bella y più grande', and, in addition – and this I must say impressed me – a caravan was likely to become extremely hot. It would be 'come un forno' in summer. The wooden house would have insulation built into its roof, and, if it didn't, we could build some in.

They varied in size and we had plenty of space for one with at least three bedrooms – far bigger than any caravan.

That night I tossed and turned more than usual on my horrible little bed. The local dogs seemed to be howling worse than ever – heralding disaster, perhaps? The wooden house seemed to make sense, and yet, an inner voice was sounding a warning note.

But night is the time for warning notes, I knew, when fears crowd in like ghosts around the bed, and even Napoleon spoke of the 'deuxième heure', when 'courage morale' is most needed.

Those bloody dogs! It wasn't just my building projects that terrified me at night. I had developed a tendency to catalogue everything that was wrong with the place: the five a.m. train that hurtled by with its piercing whistle, exactly the time when sleep might finally have come, after the dogs quietened down at four. The loudspeaker vans selling everything from politicians to brushes; the swift black snakes, supposedly harmless but nonetheless scary; the rustic rats as big as small kangaroos; the Byzantine complexity of everything, and never knowing what was going to happen next; the solitude, the idea that mafia hitmen might come creeping down the drive and do me for being foreign.

And hanging over it all the all-pervading 'problema di lingua'.

Why else was no one down here but me? I'd got it wrong, had failed to spot the obvious as usual. Had discovered paradise, but the devil was lurking behind every tree.

In the morning sunshine it was different. I walked up the drive repeating 'My house, my orchard, my beach – no one can take it away. House in the country, house by the sea, house on the beach, we've got all three.'

Then the men would arrive, big and strong and fearless, spurning my offers of caffè Inglese, seeing a joke in everything, setting my fears at rest:

'Tranquillo, Ian! Non ti preoccupare!'

For the first couple of weeks I made them coffee religiously, even buying a set of tiny cups so it seemed more like espresso. Then one day they couldn't take it any more and politeness gave way to the Italian in them. Pasquale was the first to crack. He threw his on the ground saying, 'Ian! Non buono! Caffè Inglese non buono!'

It was a relief all round.

The trip to Serra San Bruno meant an early start and a nostalgic drive back the way I'd come that day that now seemed a lifetime ago.

January in the mountains was cold, with snow on the higher peaks. The air was crisp and pine-scented as the late morning sun warmed the green canopy shading the endless succession of hairpin bends.

Serra San Bruno was as I remembered it, built on a high plateau, with a carabiniere building, the landmark given me by Gianni, as big as a communist dictator's palace. It took up a whole city block and by the time I'd driven its length three or four times, in futile search for Gianni's non-existent road, I began to get the uncomfortable feeling one gets by drawing the attention of large numbers of policemen. My car was French, my plates English and I was well out of range of the two small towns where everyone knew who I was.

So I gave up on Gianni's directions and started cruising Serra San Bruno. The keywords 'Domenico' and 'casa di legno' produced zero results for some time until, just as I was about to give up and go home, a lady in a shawl pointed up to a distant hillside saying 'case legno, molto'.

Sure enough, clustered in a field were several unmistakable examples of the casa in Gianni's picture. I made my way up a long, winding lane, coming out eventually in front of a large house overlooking the field and its strange community of show homes.

I was just in time for lunch and Domenico, small and dynamic, with a receding hairline, introduced me to his large family.

We all sat down in front of the usual huge television, without which blaring in the background Calabreses seem unable to eat. A game show was in progress, and the older and younger generations followed it keenly while Domenico and his wife concentrated on spooning out enormous portions of lunch to me, course after course.

Northern Italians refer to the south as the Mezzogiorno – The Land of Eternal Lunchtime – and I was beginning to see why. Two hours later I struggled through to Domenico's 'office', the converted front room of the house, overlooking his field full of samples. I could hardly keep my eyes open and wanted badly to sit, if not lie, down.

Domenico's manic energy, however, was undiminished, even supercharged, by the immense amounts of pasta. He rushed round the room pulling out blueprints, spreading them on tables and matching them to pictures on the walls.

When we had exhausted the possibilities of this, we headed into the field. The ones with two storeys were too large and too expensive, but Domenico wanted me to see them anyway, steep stair by steep stair. He seemed to have some idea that our relationship was destined to go further than me buying a house, into a kind of partnership, whereby mine would become a show home, famous far and wide, and the whole of southern Italy would be able to descend on me to see it.

Whether this meant giving me a discount was not clear, money being the last thing he seemed to want to talk about. I went for a single-storey three-bedder with bow windows and a front porch called 'Diana'; not absolutely the smallest and cheapest, but nearly. It measured 54 metri quadrati.

Would it fit? Domenico would be along in a few days to 'prendere le misure'. Meanwhile I was to instruct my 'operai' to do as much preliminary clearing of the site as possible.

This request, once I'd managed to get it across to them next day, was greeted with utter disdain and contempt. What business of theirs was it to assist this alien creature of the mountains? He might as well have been from Mars as far as they were concerned. A simmering hostility to the outsider Domenico developed then and there, before they'd even met him, even from Gianni, whose 'collega' I'd supposed him to be.

They don't like outsiders. I was the exception, partly because I came from so far outside it made me a curiosity too fabulous to ignore; partly because Inglesis are notoriously wealthy and seem to believe everything they are told; partly because I'd been adopted by Pino and was under his protection; but as well as this, it has to be said, without undue sentimentality, we really did get on well. Despite the problema di lingua we were a band of brothers, locked in an epic struggle to create something, none of us was quite sure what.

A few days later, Domenico arrived with a flourish in a dark blue BMW, unannounced, and as far as the 'operai' were concerned, thoroughly unwelcome. He swaggered down the drive wearing sunglasses and pointing at the unkempt strip of land next door, which he announced his intention to buy.

This was his first big mistake, excluding the BMW and sunglasses. You don't just 'buy land' around here, and anyway I wanted it myself if it ever came up. The owner is an old friend of Tralongo, one of the three original pioneers who came down here in the 1950s and converted it from farmland. No one knows where he is now; somewhere in 'The North' – in other words beyond all imagining.

But the land is a sacred trust, a useful dumping ground for all our rubbish, a tremendous resource for rats and snakes, and no one wants it not to stay that way. 'Non cambio' is the watchword here. If nothing ever changes we will all be happy. The rest of the world can change, and does change, at terrifying speed. What I had lucked into was a place that never changes and absolutely doesn't want to, and will resist all attempts to make it do so, with all its Calabrian heart. The Jasmine Coast is a place where Time stands stubbornly still.

Domenico finally got the message that he needed to cool it considerably if any headway was to be made. Far away though his home was, he was still Calabrian enough to launch a charm offensive, first in the form of cigarettes, which Pasquale quickly succumbed to.

Then he hauled his blueprints and 'Diana' picture out of the car and spread them on the roof, and curiosity did the rest. They couldn't resist the opportunity to run a critical eye over someone else's thing, and express their scepticism about this or that aspect of it. And next thing they knew they were battling through the undergrowth, measuring for all they were worth, while Domenico looked on with his blueprint, moving them about like chessmen.

By the time it was over they were fully converted, even Nino, to the idea of the casa di legno, Gianni's idea in the first place. A lot of talk ensued, too rapid for me to follow, while Pasquale puffed happily at Domenico's cigarettes. When I asked him what was going on he said, 'Tranquillo, Ian – non ti preoccupare.'

Had I but known.

What I didn't know, hadn't realised, didn't understand about building houses, was that they all, wooden or otherwise, need foundations. The idea that I didn't need to worry about it only meant 'ignorance is bliss', and I didn't stay ignorant for long. The very next day the digger was back.

Abandoning the all-important boathouse, the only thing sanctioned by architetto Napoli, they turned their full attention to digging out the foundations for the wooden one. After a while they realised that in order for them to be level they needed to create a cement apron stretching all the way from the garage to the gates. In other words the thing escalated, whereas a caravan could simply have stood on the grass.

The hole we'd dug for the boathouse could have fitted easily into this one ten times over – it was vast. It was also immensely deep, because drainage needed to be dug and a pipe laid all the way down the orchard. Conduits had to be incorporated for wiring and plumbing.

After a week of digging, and multiple deliveries of supplies on Nino di Palizzi's lorry, complete with bills, a crater had opened up big enough for an Olympic swimming pool, and we were ready for the cement lorry once more.

This time they decided to leave it in the lane behind the house and guide the giant nozzle over the back fence. My frame of mind at this point is difficult to describe: hope and despair in equal measure, I should say, with a sizeable dollop of fear. What we had done could not be undone, other than by forging ahead. There was no turning back. Sleep had become something I could only daydream about.

The cement lorry roared and the nozzle flailed like a scene from a monster movie. I stood on the bank of the pit, a helpless bystander at the unfolding catastrophe of my own life, watching my three fellow desperadoes struggle and stagger about as the grey lake slowly rose.

When there was at last a lull, another sound could be faintly heard over the idling rumble of the cement lorry: the urgent hooting of a car horn. Further investigation revealed this to be architetto Napoli, who had chosen this moment to make a site visit, stuck behind the lorry.

When he saw what was going on he flew into a rage, marched back to his car and reversed away at fantastic speed. I couldn't understand the details, but the bare facts were clear: he was going to report us to the carabiniere.

We scrambled for our phones to call Pino. Only he could head him off at the pass. Gianni got through, and I caught the words 'grandi problemi'. We stood around in a shell-shocked state for a while, before telling the cement guy to resume: after all we were doomed anyway.

'But you have no permesso for this!' Pino stood by the pit, now a glistening ocean of cement, pushing his hand back over his thick, wavy hair. The men stood around looking hangdog. Pino plainly blamed Gianni for letting it happen, and there was a stubborn slant to Gianni's normally smiling face.

'Domenico said I didn't need it, because the house is wooden.' I spoke in all our defence.

Of course Domenico would say that, and there's nothing wooden about all this cement, and anyway, 'In the south, there IS no permesso,' Pino explained with weary resignation.

'But what about what we're doing with the boathouse!' I said, becoming alarmed.

'Because of architetto Napoli the eyes will be blind.'

'And now?'

Pino shook his head. It was going to be 'molto difficile' to mollify the infuriated architetto. We would have to proceed with caution, but subito.

8

Piano Piano

The opposite to subito is piano, and piano piano is the normal speed at which things go in Calabria, unless you're driving, of course.

Like Tranquillo and Speriamo, Piano is a philosophy of life, a pace at which it is desirable, as well as inevitable, to proceed. The Calabrese do not rush into things, or if they do, as in this case, they soon slow down.

This deceleration coincided exactly with my desire to speed things up. The family were coming in August and Bunty was threatening to come in February for a site visit of her own with our old friends the Bartletts.

And the eyes of the Comune di Palizzi, I feared, might not be blind for long. It was time to get a move on.

My own eyes had been fairly blind up to now. Once opened, they viewed things with alarm. The whole place was rapidly becoming a sea of grey, under a grey sky. Sunny days were getting fewer, and whereas the Calabrese don't like working when it's too hot, they don't like working when it's raining either.

And rain it did. As Febbraio approached the heavens opened, turning our cement works into a depressing morass of puddles, and merging them in greyness with the cement driveway, paths and other grey things I hadn't noticed before.

No sun; no work being done; no one to talk to in any language; no TV; I started to feel extremely sorry for myself.

One evening I was sitting in chilly misery in the barren tiled expanse of my living room – you couldn't really call it living – longing for some furniture but unable to buy any because Bunty was trying to find a removal van in England to bring down all our junk from back to 1966 when we were married, when over the noise of the rain I thought I heard a car in the drive.

It was Pino.

I was as vulnerable to these surprise visits at night as I was in the daytime. The Calabrese have no conception of solitude and introspection. They live their lives out in the open, sociably. Someone stuck indoors on their own is someone in need of rescue, and I was that someone. The idea that I might not want to go out never occurred to them.

'A very simple ceremony' was in progress in Bova Marina, said Pino. The Festival of the Pig. It was a Men Only affair.

The Bova Marina Pig Festival was taking place in the underground garage of a half-finished apartment building just outside the town.

'The women have been cooking the pig for four days,' Pino explained on the way. 'After this the skin is a great delicacy.'

The men of Bova were seated in rows at trestle tables, as tough a bunch of customers as I've ever seen. They all looked up as Pino produced me at the doorway, like a very reluctant rabbit out of a hat.

'Presento Inglese Ian,' he announced.

A ripple went round the room, not exactly hostile, but not exactly overjoyed to see me either, I couldn't help thinking. The only person who was pleased was Davide, who took me under his youthful wing and dragged me off to join a small group of what turned out to be Chelsea supporters.

Bottles of wine and bottles of Sprite lined the tables. Whether this vile combination was part of the custom of the pig ceremony I never knew, but a plastic beaker was set before me and filled with the mixture. The Chelsea supporters raised theirs to me with a chorus of 'Salutis!' then stared at me intently.

I knocked mine back. It was the best way; swiftness masked the taste, followed by a slight warm glow. It was refilled immediately. In the south a man's manhood can be gauged by his capacity for drink.

The only thing my new friends knew about the English was gathered from the behaviour of Chelsea supporters.

Something between cross-examination and downright interrogation then ensued, a conversational style I was getting used to. It seems aggressive, especially if the subject is the impassioned one of football, but really it's just another version of the Calabrese unaffected manner. They are all Republicans without really knowing it, just as they are Catholics who know their 'Papa' lives in Rome. They are mannered, but without the bother of middle-class manners. They tell it like it is, or ask it ('demandare' is the word for ask) with no frills.

I finally confessed that I was born in Chelsea and live nearby but support QPR. It seemed a good way of heading them off because, as I had guessed, none of them had heard of QPR.

Queens Park Rangers is my local club, and for a while we had a family membership and stood in the cold yelling 'Come on you Rs' with the same slight sense of hopelessness as the rest of the crowd. I enjoyed it, and the hamburgers we munched to keep ourselves warm, but beyond that my knowledge of football is pretty well nil. I didn't want this to become apparent to my new friends.

'Why you not support Chelsea?'

I was struggling for a diplomatic reply to this when someone at another table shouted 'Manchester United!' Another yelled 'Juventus!' and a fight broke out. I was saved from my embarrassment, but the atmosphere was definitely hotting up.

Whether the womenfolk sensed this, or it was pure coincidence, they chose this moment to file into the room with platters piled with boiled pig, and violence was temporarily averted. Everybody got stuck in, and my football dilemma was replaced by a plastic plateful of greasy pork.

The Chelsea fans watched me tackle it with the same hawk-like intensity, fascinated to know how an Inglese might rise to this challenge. There was no doubt the whole English nation was depending on me, and the waters of Cape Trafalgar and the field of Waterloo, not to mention the playing fields of Eton, were reduced to a cement basement in Bova Marina.

'England Expects' about summed it up, and with this in mind I stuck my plastic fork into a wobbling jelly-like lump and swallowed it. Again, speed was of the essence, and the wine-Sprite cocktail came in handy as a lubricant. Which was the skin delicacy and which the flesh I never discovered.

The fighting became more general after the feast, and it began to dawn on me that there was more to this festival than I'd thought. I knew Pino was running for mayor of Bova and I now realised that this was a gathering of local political factions, not unlike the Blues and Greens of Ancient Rome.

And like the Blues and Greens they expressed themselves forcefully. Inflamed by pig and wine spritzer they soon came to blows. The women calmly removed the detritus of the meal as the men set to. Chairs hit the ground, then bodies. I saw Pino discreetly disappear into a back room, but his eleven-year-old son Davide was in the thick of it. Child though he was, I saw him land a back headbutt on a youth twice his size, causing blood to flow.

At this point I decided it was time to leave. Like anyone in my position might, I'd viewed developments, first with surprise, then with increasing alarm. How long could it be before these toughs joined forces against the common enemy?

For the moment even my Chelsea friends had lost interest in me, and I slipped away unnoticed into the night. I found Pino's car unlocked (crime down here tends to be organised) and climbed in.

I must have fallen asleep because the next thing I knew we were cruising along the coast road. The weather had cleared, the sky was full of stars over the dark sea and a creamy line of white ran along the shoreline. Pino had his window open and the smell of the pines rushed in with the cool night air.

'A very simple ceremony,' said Pino.

I thought it as good a way as any of describing it.

*

That night, unbeknownst to me, the unfurnished condition of my life had made a deep impression on Pino, and a few evenings later he was back. This time we drove to his house in Bova, collected Celeste and the children, and continued on to the slightly larger town Melito Porto Salvo. It was to be an outing for me.

It was my first experience, but by no means my last, of the kind of restaurant Pino and clearly lots of other people in our little 'Altro Mondo', really like.

In England we tend to think of Italian restaurants as small, intimate places, at the most trattorias, with plenty of terracotta, gleaming tiles and white-aproned waiters. Places of warm, subtle comfort and convivial dining.

Probably they are like that in Rome, and I'm not saying they don't exist down here, but for choice the Calabrese prefer their restaurants large. By that I mean huge, barn-like places that go on for miles, room after room. Enormous televisions blare down at you from high places, with deafeningly loud football matches and game shows.

The evening meal starts late, and goes on forever, despite the extreme youth and extreme age of many of the diners. Very few people go out to dinner in Calabria without their entire famiglia in tow, at least three generations.

Pino seemed to know everyone in the place, and we slowly progressed from family to family, greeting to greeting, room to room, until at last we were in a relatively empty one, very brightly lit, where we sat down at a table right in the middle.

The arrival of plates piled with bread was very welcome, and as the seventeen or so antipasti, gli spaghetti ai carciofi, pesce stocco mollicato, testina di agnello al forno, and the crowning glory, cinghiale dell' aspromonte, went down, washed by wine, followed by assorted dolci and gelati, topped off with caffè and limoncello, I was pretty relaxed by the end of it.

Children at tables all around us were falling asleep, and my own eyelids were distinctly heavy, when Pino announced that the time had come to find Ian some furniture at his friend Signor Pizzi's store. I struggled to object, but was too relaxed and felt too obligated to do so.

Mobile Pizzi was still open, and, like the restaurant, incredibly vast. Room after room of interminable furniture stretched before my weary eyes.

Signor Pizzi, dapper, prosperous, welcomed us effusively. I'm not saying it was a set-up exactly, but he was definitely expecting us. It was almost midnight and the store was otherwise empty.

Laden with brochures I started to wander the aisles. Bright strip lighting shimmered off the shiny surfaces, which typified Signor Pizzi's taste, adding a weird kind of snow-blindness to my disoriented condition.

I don't know much about furniture – I can't even say I know what I like. I like what Bunty likes. She is a Bohemian aristocrat to her fingertips, with an eye for the exquisite and offbeat second to none. She grew up in splendid historic houses, both distressed and otherwise, stuffed with beautiful things, in an aura of faded grandeur and shabby chic.

I, on the other hand, haven't got a clue. I grew up in Weybridge and it shows. I've been trying to escape suburbia all my life, but it's hard to take it out of the boy. Now here I was in deepest provincial Italy, dangerously close to becoming the slaughtered lamb.

It's an odd thing that in this land of Michaelangelo and Gianni Versace (who came from Reggio Calabria) you can't find a decent bed. That's what I thought after pounding the aisles for a while at Mobile Pizzi.

I didn't have anywhere to lie down comfortably, which I longed to do, or sit on and watch television if only I had a television. So, conscious though I was of the dangers, I was pretty motivated, not to mention lubricated. I examined every bed in the place, longing for one to be something not immensely heavy, grotesquely elaborate, hideously shinily new and wildly expensive.

Then Viviana came up with the 'Divano'. They were displayed in a different section and she'd found one she liked.

Glad to escape from the beds, I followed her obediently, to find the others grouped round a large lump wrapped in plastic. Pizzi was tearing it off.

I was so tired it was a relief to sit down on anything, and this was my undoing. My relief was taken for approval and next thing I knew I'd bought the thing. Pizzi, scribbling furiously on his pad, asked me what colour, and Viviana whispered in my ear that her favourite colour was orange.

And so the Orange Divano came into our lives, a ponderous monument to the foolishness of men who make impulsive decisions when the wine is red.

Next morning, in the cold light of day, I kept telling myself that at least I'd have something to sit on. Or perhaps it wouldn't look as bad as all that.

But it did, in fact quite a lot worse, and by the time Pizzi's van headed back up the drive I was 2,000 euros the poorer.

It took five strong Calabrese to unload the beast – it seemed to be made of something heavier than lead – and the cushions, when I sat on them, were the same. Some expert in discomfort had contrived the thing. The back pushed you forwards and downwards, and the hard cushions pushed you back up. There simply wasn't any position in which you could kick back and say 'Aaahhh'.

I tried pulling out the base to make a bed, which perhaps might justify my expenditure. After much arm-wrenching and knuckle-grazing a thin thing unfurled – more of a mat than a mattress. When you lay on it metal springs and other sharp things dug into you, and your head disappeared under the sofa-back. And the rock-hard cushions, removed from the base, had nowhere to go. The awful truth was, try as I might not to face it, Tralongo's sagging singles were comfier.

The thing dominated the bare living space like an orange colossus

– immovable, defiant almost, its back against the wall, and Bunty arriving any minute.

Worst of all it was non-returnable. There was no way back from the catastrophe without causing offence all round that might permanently blight my Calabrian future.

So the following day, when they all came to admire it, the Pino and the Pizzi families – Signora Pizzi wearing the most fabulous diamond and emerald earrings, I couldn't help noticing – I had to pretend to love the beastly thing.

'Bellissima!'

Meanwhile, outside in the rain, progress was piano indeed. The men would arrive, shelter disconsolately for a while, then leave when they'd finished their takeaway espressos.

They abandoned the bleak wooden house foundations for the boathouse, where they could sit under cover.

Then one day the sun came out and gave Pasquale an idea – the 'idea di genius di testicolo di Pasquale', as Gianni called it, and as it has been known ever since.

This was to build a flat roof.

In Italy the idea is not unique – that if you have a roof and you live somewhere sunny, which you do, then why not make it flat – in other words, a terrazzo.

I liked the idea immediately, but we all knew that in the skitch the roof sloped. The idea of further inflaming architetto Napoli was inadvisable, but asking him to change it in his present mood was probably futile.

Gianni and Pasquale finally convinced me it was most unlikely we'd be seeing Napoli in the foreseeable future, and when we did it would probably only be when he'd simmered down.

So we ditched the last vestige of the skitch and started laying out a wide, splendid roof terrace, which would have sea views stretching for miles.

My next 2,000 euros went on a television. Unable to stand the long evenings alone with the divano, I decided to round it off with something I could sit and watch, or at a pinch curl up uncomfortably and watch. I had made my bed, as they say, and had to do my best to lie in it.

Pino had a cousin in Bova with a TV store, and though there was one much nearer in Brancaleone, I naturally went with cousin Carmello. He drove out to the house and regaled me with a lot of technical jargon, the gist of which was that I needed a dish.

The 'sistema' of this dish meant downing tools at the boathouse for a lot of critical standing around by Gianni and co. Carmello and his assistant were never short of advice. Hoisting it up meant more active participation.

Cement was needed, ladders borrowed, ropes and tackle pulled upon. Finally the huge eyesore was up and the mood became festive.

'Televisione di Ian. Bravo.'

The televisione itself was carried into the house like a particularly large trophy after a battle. It took all six of us. It was the biggest television I'd ever seen, like a megalithic monster with one giant cycloptic eye. Rigging up its wiring took the rest of the day, but by that evening I was hooked up to Sky Italia and my life was changed.

Next day it rained and there was no progress, but I had six Sky movie channels and an English language option. I curled up happily on the orange monster, its lumpiness counteracted by a massive overdose of telly.

I was getting used to the Calabrese pace-of-life option too. Once you get acclimatised and forget you're from northern Europe and the Big City, with all its urgency and stress, the Mezzogiorno Magic starts to take hold and the 'piano, piano' pace seems the only one that makes any sense: work to live, rather than live to work. All the rest is propaganda.

9

Costa Nostra

Domenico wanted me to meet him in Reggio one evening to sign the contract and finalise things. We met in the bar of a large old-fashioned hotel on the lungomare, looking out across the railway tracks at the Straits of Messina, a view which could vie with the Bay of Naples but doesn't, because the powers-that-be refuse to beautify it as it deserves.

Sometimes the stubborn philistinism of the Calabrese, incomprehensible and self-defeating, overwhelms the rustic charm that almost excuses it. The seafront at Reggio is a classic example, where a beautiful promenade could so easily be built for leisurely strolling – la passeggiata – on balmy evenings. But there isn't one, and I rarely go there except to catch the train to Naples, four hours away, where you can gaze at their beautiful bay and get your pocket picked into the bargain.

Domenico had my personal plans spread out on a bar room table, showing how my Diana house would fit on our foundations when it eventually arrived from Romania.

'And when will that be?' I asked.

Domenico shrugged expressively. 'There are many ships from Romania to Vibo Valentia!'

'And which one will my Diana be on?'

'First we must send money.'

Ah. I'd been wondering when this would come up. Seven thousand five hundred more of my euros, half the price of the casa di legno, roofed and glazed but bare, to be plumbed and wired by me, needed to be paid upfront to set things in motion. When it arrived a team of Romanians would arrive with it and erect it in ten days.

'But first your own operai must prepare the basis with the wires and tubes from this drawings.'

I gave him a cheque drawn on my new bank, the Banca dei Monti Paschi di Siena, 'the oldest bank in the world', whose direttore was a friend of Pino's. At our brief meeting he'd given me a credit card, told me not to worry if my account was red or black – 'what is the difference?' – and asked me if I supported Chelsea.

'QPR,' I said.

Next day Gianni and co. looked grimly at the drawings, which did nothing to diminish their dislike of Domenico.

'È necessario romperle,' was the verdict. 'Romperle grande, e dopo più cemento.'

Not dig the whole thing up, exactly, but enough of it to make us all want to bury Domenico in the next load of cement.

'Casa di legno malo idea,' said Nino, shaking his head.

'Idea di Gianni,' said Pasquale.

It was all Gianni's fault.

But at least it was 'non urgente' – none of us expected the wooden house to arrive any time soon. 'Piano piano' was the watchword as usual. The alto terrazzo – 'idea di Pasquale' – was our new priority.

Next up was Franco from Condofuri, whose wife was a friend, or possibly a cousin, of Pasquale's wife.

Condofuri is one step beyond Bova Marina, not strictly speaking on our map, but in this case it had to be because Franco's 'Vivaio' was there, the only garden centre known to sell cypressas.

Cypress pines had been a dream of mine from the start, to give the place the Tuscan touch it lacked – a classical whiff of Ancient Rome. I wanted to line the back fence with them, with maybe a few dotted along the drive. No self-respecting Italian palazzo lacks cypressas, mixed ideally with umbrella pines and date palms, and I'd been thinking for some time that the key to folie de grandeur lay in the garden. The villa itself was only a bungalow, and despite its Tardis-like interior it always would be.

Franco turned out to be a large, overwhelming person, who called me 'Ross', hugged me like a bear, then wandered down the drive saying 'Eden!' repeatedly.

Cypress pines – classico alto – cost a hundred euros each and I needed fourteen of them, but as the morning gathered pace it turned out that other beautiful trees, as well as plants, were needed to achieve my dream, and could easily be supplied by Franco.

The fence along the drive would be lined with bamboo, at thirty-five euros per plant, forming the backdrop for a row of cycas palms, male and female, interspersed between my existing umbrella pines. The cycas, short-trunked and notoriously expensive, would be at eye-height for visitors in cars. Franco thought this would create a good first impression. Every so often they sprout extraordinary flowering cones and megasporophylls, and I felt my resistance crumbling. It was the same with yuccas, date palms and the tall, Washingtonia 'skydusters'. Such palms could transform the place overnight. It was only a question of money.

Mature fruit trees don't come cheap either, but on the other hand the idea of instant oranges and lemons, not to mention mandarins, was one that Franco, despite the language difficulty, was able to elaborate most eloquently. And anyway I was sold in the first place, a soft touch that the likes of Franco can normally only dream of.

He admired our 'works', especially those in progress on the alto terrazzo, and generally involved himself as a full participant, with words of advice for all. Then he wrote my order down at great length in his book. When I asked him what it was all going to cost he became vague, as is always the way with the Calabrese, until the final coup de grâce.

Next morning a truck arrived, driven by two robust Albanese, loaded to the brim with tropical pot plants, none of which had even been mentioned, never mind ordered. 'For the alto terrazzo,' one of the Albanese explained.

I should've been shocked, alarmed, warned at least about Franco, but I was only amused at the sheer audacity of it. It was an outrageous try-on, but he must have thought the odds worth the trip. I might have said yes – I had to everything else.

I said no, and the truck went away. The incident was never mentioned and next day the truck was back, driven by the same Albanese, this time loaded with digging equipment. They set to, filling the place with enormous holes. The cypressas arrived a few days later, accompanied by a 'maestro di alberi', who I suspect supplied them to Franco.

Franco came as well, Gianni and co. downed tools, and the ceremonial planting began. As with olive trees, the ritual of planting cypressa pines is taken very seriously, and they must be exactly three metres apart. Soon the back fence along the lane was majestically lined with twelve magnificent cypressas, plus one extra tall one by the gate.

The feeling of being able to enhance nature, to alter landscape at will with trees and achieve a vision, to harmonise in spirit with Capability Brown and Louis XIV, drove all other considerations, such as money, completely from my mind. Trees plus labour plus compost plus fertiliser plus whatever came to 2,000 euros. In my Sun King mood it seemed the merest bagatelle.

Next day it started raining in earnest and all work ceased. It was as if the gods were issuing some celestial reprimand about my classical pretensions. All over the garden the crater-like holes filled with water and the huge piles of earth added to the general impression of the Battle of the Somme. And this is how it looked when Bunty arrived.

I'd known she was coming, of course, just not that the place would be looking its absolute worst. We'd already decided it was uninhabitable, with our friends Rosie and Tony in tow, so I'd booked us all rooms at the San Giorgio, to the great joy of the Signora. Maybe the sun would come out before they got here.

For some reason they flew to Naples, then caught the train, and I drove into Reggio to meet them. But when the train pulled into Stazione Centrale there was no sign of them.

I didn't know what to do, or who to ask, but I'd brought my mobile phone for once, and when I got back in the car it rang. 'We're in Sicily!' a faint voice said.

They'd managed to be in the wrong half of the train when it split at Villa San Giovanni, and the next thing they knew they were afloat. Now they were in Messina, trying to get back.

It seemed pointless to try to meet them, since they didn't know where they might land or when, so I headed for the San Giorgio on my own. The idea was that they'd call me if they ever reached the mainland, and I would direct them from there. Not a good start whichever way you looked at it. Meanwhile I felt rather like a prisoner on release, buzzing along the coast to my holiday hotel instead of my usual solitary confinement.

Things were in a heightened state of preparation for the moglie and amici of the 'vagabondo', as the Signora calls me, and although in February there were no guests, quite a large welcoming party was gathered. I had great difficulty explaining to the Signora that they weren't here yet, and why, and that they would be arriving soon – 'Speriamo'.

I went to our table-of-honour in the dining room, and sat there dunking bread in vino locale for a couple of hours, while the Italians returned to their usual, apparently never-ending, TV game show.

At last my phone rang and they were on their way, which Bunty had remembered. It was just for the last bit that I needed to go out to the roadside and flag down their taxi.

After several unsuccessful attempts, and nearly getting run over a couple of times, the right car slowed down and pulled in.

Tony and Rosie Bartlett are our best friends. We used to double-date before we were married, back in the rosy mists of the sixties. Tony is everything I'm not – rich, successful, businesslike, hard-working – yet we get on. We both like Elvis, who radically altered our worldview when we were teenagers. It's an ideal sort of friendship really: we don't see each other that often, and can say what we like when we do, without being bothered about each other's feelings.

Tony is a builder and I had a nasty feeling he was about to exercise this custom pretty freely when he saw what was afoot at Villa La Buntessa. And La Buntessa herself was much more likely to listen to him than to me.

After a chilly night we convened for a merry breakfast on the Signora's terrace. It wasn't actually raining, and the Signora produced cappuccinos, with jugs of extra espresso and frothy milk, plates piled with brioches and cornetti, jars of home-made marmallata and big chunks of butter. It was all extremely unhealthy and delicious.

The main topic of conversation was still whose fault it was they'd ended up in Sicily. According to the women Tony's; according to him, theirs. I sided with him, partly through male bonding, partly in the hope that he might side with me in the near future. Feelings of anxiety were beginning to interfere with my breakfast.

The moment finally came when we piled into the Clio and set off on the short drive to what I knew might well be my doom. I found myself justifying things – the weather, the shabbiness of Galati, the choices I'd made or been forced to make – I hadn't realised till then how nervous I was.

As we trundled along our bumpy lane Bunty started justifying too – how wonderfully rustic it all was, how much we liked trains – but she soon stopped when she saw the cypressas.

They were very much the first impression a person got; slender incongruous pencils of green standing out like sore forefingers against the shabby Calabrian shrubbery. Bunty called them 'depressas' – 'like being in a chuchyard'. The persistent rain undoubtedly heightened this impression.

'That's yews – they're not yews, anyone can see that.'

'They're still depressing whatever they are.'

It wasn't a good start, and once through the gates the full impact of the wooden house foundations hit us like a blow. Even I was struck by how vast and grey they were.

'My God! What have you done! It used to be so lovely up here! So wild and overgrown! You've ruined it!'

'It was overgrown with weeds and full of nasty red beetles. It had to be cleared, even if we just had a caravan.'

'Parked on the grass, like the professore's, not on this helipad!'

'It isn't a helipad and it isn't for a caravan – we've had a better idea.'

'Oh, God, Ian – what have you done?'

I must admit I was beginning to wonder myself. I tried to explain about the wooden house, and how cheap it was, compared to a caravan. Well, compared to a proper house, anyway. Tony said with foundations like these we could build a skyscraper.

Things didn't improve, as I'd hoped they might, when we got nearer the sea, away from the World War One no-man's-land our orchard had become. Gianni and the team were at work, preparing the flat roof for the massive reinforcement of cement needed to turn it into a terrace, and I thought they might cheer things up a bit. They usually do. They scrambled down their ladder to be 'presented', but they were on their best behaviour and not in the right mood for their usual joking.

Rosie and Tony admired the view and gazed about the place with a mixture of awe and bewilderment. They shook hands with Gianni, Pasquale and Nino, and so did Bunty, who hadn't met them before. I felt oddly torn between the two groups – my wife and my oldest friends versus my new ones, with whom my loyalties now lay. The idea that we must stand together against the foreigner, who might well not understand our ways, was definitely in the air.

One thing Tony didn't understand was how we were planning to get up onto this marvellous roof terrace.

'You hadn't thought of that, had you?'

I hadn't. None of us had.

My visitors then made a great meal of inspecting the boathouse interior, pointing out all the places you couldn't put stairs. Gianni and co. became taciturn when the undeniable truth became clear, while I gravitated between the groups, searching for a solution, trying to keep it light, as if it was just a detail.

Pasquale saved the day by inventing impromptu a flight of 'scala esterna' that faced the drive, then turned at right angles along the back fence, to a point at the corner of what was, after all, his terrace.

'Perfetto.'

It seemed like I'd got away with it, but the damage was done, and confidence in my management skills was fatally undermined.

'What are all those huge holes for?' Bunty asked.

'Just some trees.'

'And what are they costing?'

I wasn't sure, just as I wasn't sure what Gianni and co. were costing per day, what the materials had come to so far, what the total cost of the wooden house was likely to be, including foundations, etc.

At this point the cement lorry arrived, in all its extravagant pink-and-green hugeness, ripping off branches on its merry way. And what was *that* costing?

The atmosphere in the car was strained when we at last left the building site for a spin in the countryside. Bunty was on the lookout for old shutters to detach from derelict houses to 'distress' the boat-house, determined to save what she could of her dear little cottage from the wreck of my grandiose folly. It's true the increased size and flat roof had given the place a somewhat palatial air. This hadn't been my intention, but it was no use telling them that.

The weather continued cold and grey, rendering everything dismal. The Jasmine Coast gets 326 days of sunshine a year, and this wasn't one of them. When it isn't sunny the whole place becomes bleaker than an English seaside resort out of season. The arid climate and dodgy architecture combine to depress the visitor. The chalk-faced hillsides turn grimy, as do the beaches, where flotsam and jetsam from passing ships tends to accumulate in winter.

There was nothing I could say. I didn't have the heart, and my credibility was shot.

We drove through Brancaleone, where a light drizzle added the final dampener to our spirits.

'Perhaps we could find somewhere for lunch?' I said, but the one and only restaurant was closed.

'Let's go up into the mountains,' said Tony, 'there's bound to be something there.'

But what? My experience of the mountains was of small, isolated towns with narrow streets where people brood on ancient vendettas and stare at you. The idea of the kind of restaurant they had in mind was as remote as the town Tony spotted, clinging to a peak high above the rolling hills behind Brancaleone.

Rosie said, 'And we're bound to find some old shutters there.'

The road wound up and up, its surface gradually deteriorating. After a while a large villa appeared through some trees. Bunty called out, 'Stop, stop!'

Imposing old gates hung open, weeds grew in the rustic stone courtyard and plenty of broken-looking shutters dangled from tall peeling window fames.

'What do you think?' said Bunty.

Rosie said, 'It *looks* empty.'

'Those shutters are fantastic.'

'Who's going to go?' I said.

'You are,' said Bunty.

'Oh, no. I've got to drive. In case we need to make a quick getaway.'

'Which we very well might,' said Tony. 'I think you're all mad.'

The villa, though down-at-heel, was a classical gem, and the gardens, though overgrown, were full of flowers and vegetables.

'Tony might be right,' I said. 'I'm not sure it's empty.'

'Of course it's empty,' said Rosie. 'There isn't a sign of life.'

'I'm going to go,' said Bunty. 'If anyone comes I'll just pretend I didn't realise.'

She left the car, crossed the courtyard and started tugging at a shutter. A dog started barking and five women came rushing out of the house.

'Told you,' said Tony.

I started the engine and Bunty, pursued by the women and the barks, if not the actual dog, raced to the car and jumped in just as I roared off.

'Phew!' I said. 'That was close.'

Rosie said, 'It *looked* empty.'

And Tony said, 'Well it wasn't.'

The streets of the little mountain town were even narrower than I'd feared, the houses either side tilting towards each other, almost touching. Once committed there was no turning back, and we pressed on towards whatever lay in store at the heart of the place. A priest was talking to a group of black-clad women outside a church. They stopped and stared as we drove by towards a small central piazza.

Umbrella ficus were planted neatly round the perimeter, where parking spaces were marked out in front of another church. We parked and got out, and looked around, like spacemen landing on a strange planet.

No charming little restaurant with umbrella-shaded tables greeted our gaze, but up some steps to a high pavement a bar tabacceria looked open, if not particularly inviting.

'We can have lunch there,' said Tony.

Behind the bar a shelf was packed with an astonishing array of winged football trophies, and packed around the walls on a bench a group of old men, perhaps the elders of the village who in their youth had scored all those goals, stopped whatever they were doing to gaze silently at the four foreigners. There was no sign of any food.

Tony ordered a beer. It seemed the right thing to do, and might have defrosted the atmosphere, but didn't. To make matters worse Bunty and Rosie wanted Perrier.

I said, 'Caffè, per favore,' and pointed my fingers at my mouth and said, 'Mangiare?'

The pale-skinned woman behind the bar shook her head with absolute finality, before pulling my espresso in a marked manner. We weren't going to make friends here, that was obvious, and it was a relief to knock back our drinks and bid them all a final 'Ciao'.

We got to the car definitely wanting to escape, but the only way out was the way we'd come in. We'd gone a few yards when round the bend ahead came a funeral procession, led by the priest we'd seen earlier, accompanied by a mournful brass band. We had no option but to reverse and become the unwilling focal point of the mourners as they entered the square.

Incense bearers followed the priest, and a youth with a banner bearing the name of the deceased: Don Philippo Calvino.

Bunty grabbed my arm, 'There you are. Look.'

'Look at what?'

'He's a Don,' she hissed.

'That doesn't mean anything,' I said.

'Of *course* it does!'

'What about Don Quixote? Was *he* a mafioso?'

'Don't be ridiculous! What do you think, Tony?'

'I think we'll be lucky to get out of this place alive.'

'Well *you* wanted to come here,' said Rosie.

The procession finally moved into the piazza church and we made our getaway. I drove down the mountain as fast as the rain and the hairpins and the potholes would allow.

Lunchtime and mezzogiorno were long gone by the time I remembered the hillside restaurant where we'd celebrated my acquisition that day, what now seemed an aeon ago, before the words 'sempre problemi' had entered my slender Italian vocabulary.

'There is a place,' I said. 'I don't know if it's open this time of year, or this time of day.' It was four o'clock, when most things are still chiuso.

Packed inside steamy windows and looking out on the sodden Astroturf where, in summer sunshine, I'd sat celebrating before, didn't do much to dispel the mood of pessimism that had replaced the optimism of those days, as suspect fish and abject failure were picked over in the fuggy, claustrophobic atmosphere.

The place was surprisingly full, mainly of male groups lingering over the last stages of lengthy lunches. I wasn't sure how pleased the Signora was to see a new group starting at that hour, though she put on a brave show of welcoming and remembering me, the important English friend of Dottore Pino Toscano.

Tony was sure it was a fish restaurant, or if not should be, on this famously fishy shore. I knew better, but no one would listen, my credibility by then being nil. Fish wasn't 'consigliato' that day, and with her huge menu I thought it unwise to deviate, especially at late afternoon when resources and staff would be minimal.

The local fish in February is an acquired taste anyway: some squid-like bottom feeder – called alici, I think – they all love, which I tried once and which tasted almost as bad as the boiled pig.

When it came, Tony said his was 'warmed over', but this was impossible for me to translate, since I only knew the word 'caldo', meaning hot. Anyway I didn't want to complain.

'You would have it,' I said. 'My rigatoni's delicious.'

That night at the San Giorgio the awful consequences were wreaked on my visitors, driving the final nail into the coffin of anything good they might have thought about Calabria. The warmed-over fish returned to haunt them in horrible, heaving, green-faced waves.

'That woman ought to be prosecuted,' Tony moaned in weak-voiced outrage.

Next morning I left them all in bed, pale and whimpering. When I got to the house, where I'd hoped to find a bit of peace, I found Pino remonstrating with the men. They were managing to look sheepish and defiant at the same time. I wondered what the trouble was now.

The trouble was the alto terrazzo. Pino spread his arms in sema-phore-like dismay towards the splendid sea view of which we were all so proud. The problem, it was gradually borne in on me, was the splendid view it gave of *us* from the point of view of the coastguard – the Caribinieri del Mare – who constantly patrolled the coast, on the lookout for illegal building. I'd seen a grey customs cutter creaming by from time to time, and rather admired it's MTB-like lines, little knowing it was a dangerous predator.

We had gone a level too far, in Pino's opinion, exposing ourselves to 'grande rischi': 'The sea has eyes!' said Pino.

From now on a watch would have to be kept at all times, the

horizon swept through my father's WW2 binoculars, and tools downed at the first sign of the coastguard cutter.

It was all rather exciting, and when he'd gone we joked about it. All the same, it was only now I realised that what I was doing was totally illegal. And I could hardly have chosen a more exposed place to do it. Right there on the beach the boathouse stuck out like a sore thumb.

Next day my visitors were feeling better and wanted to go into Reggio. The weather had improved – at least it wasn't actually raining. It was a relief to take a break from the damp Jasmine Coast.

Bunty had got it into her head that somewhere in the hive-like bustle of this densely packed city we would find a shop which sold a traditional Sicilian high-cut jacket suitable for me to wear at the forthcoming wedding of my daughter Mia.

'Like you see pictures of old men wearing' was all she would say to illustrate the object of our quest. 'You know.'

We didn't know, and nor did the many bewildered shopkeepers we hunted down, gathering round them like wolves, gesturing and describing something we were far from clear about ourselves. Sicily was in plain sight across the water, and we kept pointing to it, but to no avail.

I had a sort of nineteenth-century image in my head – possibly a memory from *The Leopard* – black with plenty of satin and a cravat secured with a pearl stickpin – but nothing even remotely like that was on display in any of the many windows we gazed into, even if that was what she meant. Deep down I was pretty sure we were in the wrong city for anything so stylish. Palermo perhaps, or Rome, but definitely not Reggio.

By the time both we and the possibilities were exhausted we had walked miles, and had seen pretty well all there was to see of Reggio – the giant trees along the lungomare, where all the nice cafés should be but aren't; the waterfront where the promenade is occupied by railway tracks instead of strollers; the Norman castle frowning down; the museum where the magnificent Hellenic bronzes, incongruous in the amateur theatrical atmosphere of such a provincial setting, stare sightlessly from their Attic past at the thin trickle of gaping tourists struggling to imagine the remote world of such impassive, heroic giants.

We'd worked our way back to the streets around the parking zone of the Stazione Centrale, tired and hungry, the mezzogiorno having long since passed, when we were brought up short by the surprising sight of a MacDonald's. Open all day, about as un-Italian as it could be, it drew us into its familiar ambience, rich with fast food fragrances, much as one of those ancient Greek heroes might have been drawn by a Temple of Diana.

In London we might have been too green-minded and snooty for MacDonald's, but here its appeal seemed almost exotic, particularly in view of our recent treatment at the hands of the Lucrezia Borgia of Spropoli.

We sat in a window booth, up to our elbows in Big Macs, fries and thick, gooey milkshakes that first went down like nectar, then off like bombs in the interior regions. We were feeling extremely happy and guilty, when it dawned on us that an anti-war demo was going on in the street outside.

As the cavalcade moved slowly away, we were left staring across the empty street, with its detritus, the litter of protest, gently stirring over the flattened cobbles into the gutters. The opposite pavement for the first time was revealed. Diagonally across from us, taking up fully half a block, was the most gleaming, modern, post-modern, direct from Rome and Milan, Designer Italian Kitchen store.

An Italian kitchen! Of course! Why hadn't she thought of that before? Exactly what that sorry little bungalow needed! Bunty herself now became a convert to Destino. She was up and out of the door and across the street before the rest of us could properly digest what was going on.

We finished up and followed, entering the hushed, expensive, richly carpeted temple of Italian design – glowing woods, rich dark plastics, deeply polished stainless steel surfaces – just as she was taking a nosegay of glossy brochures from a handsome, obsequious, gallant Italian salesperson.

'Come and look over here!' she called across the brilliantly lit interior space – a woman literally reborn. 'You won't believe this!'

The kitchens were displayed in their own mini-showrooms, where their multiple options could be explained and priced by the handsome Italian, and it was in one of these that we found the Veneta Cocina. It spoke to us all right away. This was Art! This was Beauty! The Veneta Cocina was the direct descendant of the Renaissance by way of the sixties. The colours were rich and the drawers slid shut with a slow, quiet thump, like the door of a chauffeur-driven Rolls Royce.

Bunty chose a 'run' in white and red with polished aluminium trim that we all thought should fit one way or another. Someone from the fitting team would come and take exact measurements.

It looked like we were in for a bill knocking on for 15,000 euros. It was going to make a big hole in whatever might be left of the 50,000 euros, but who was counting? Certainly not Bunty. She'd made the transition from cautious to reckless as only she can. There's opulence in her aristocratic blood that rushes to the surface from time to time, and this was one of them.

When we got back we grouped in the villa, gazing at the bleak expanse of chilly tiles, each of us imagining how beautiful it was going to be, transformed by the Veneta Cocina.

As it was, the orange divano glared grimly at the giant TV, like two heavyweight boxers in a pre-fight standoff. Despite their size they only seemed to increase the sense of emptiness.

Nobody had really said anything about the divano, but I knew what they were all thinking. Now Rosie suddenly turned to it and with a surge of unexpected optimism said, 'You know, you can do wonders with a throw.'

That was pretty much her final word on Calabria, and next day I took them to the station to catch the Eurostar to Naples. As they climbed aboard their comfortable compartment I felt a sudden wave of homesick loneliness at being left behind. I stood on the platform till the train was out of sight. What madness had driven me to exile in this place that made Alice's Wonderland seem normal?

10

The Sea Has Eyes

February ended at last with a flurry of tree-planting by Franco. He arrived with two truckloads and a bill for 13,000 euros. This time there was no sending back, though how he had arrived at so vast a sum was never satisfactorily explained.

On the other hand the sun came out, the holes were filled in, the trees looked splendid, March was upon us, and with it spring and that perennial hope of rebirth that keeps mankind from shooting itself every year.

The little fishing boats were back, puttering about on the blue water, and I watched them busying themselves with things that since time immemorial have gone on in this place, while keeping a weather eye out for the carabinieri of the sea.

One day, off-watch, I was pottering about in the orchard, pouring water on the new banana palms, when a small blue car appeared at the gates, paused, then made its way slowly down the drive. As if in slow motion the details of this vehicle gradually impacted on my brain: the little blue light on the roof; the word 'Carabinieri' in red letters down the side.

The sheer horror of what was happening paralysed me at first, rooting me to the spot. They hadn't come from the sea! I'd been taken in the rear! Like Napoleon at Waterloo, it was the old story of the sunken road. Like the Brits in Singapore my guns had been pointing the wrong way.

I remember thinking 'That's it! I'm finished! The Dream has died today!'

Biting the bullet as best I could I set off to face the music. Knowing I was doomed was in a way helpful, because it produced the sort of fatalistic calm which I suppose helps condemned men walking to their place of execution stay brave until the last.

Arranging my face into what I hoped was a confident, casual smile I emerged from the cover of the house into what you might call the scene of the crime. There were two carabinieri, one waiting for me by the car, the other up on the alto terrazzo, talking into a mobile phone. Their immaculate uniforms blazed in the sun, vivid against the damning evidence of illegal works. Of the men there was no sign. They had flown like birds.

'Is there a problem, officer?' I said, my invariable opening gambit with members of the Force. I was counting on innocence and the language barrier coming to my aid.

'Are there some people working here?' the carabiniere said, in perfect English.

'No, no – not as far as I can see.'

'Whose cars are these?' All three of the fugitives' cars were parked on the grass beside us.

'Erm – oh, those are some friends of mine.'

'Friends of yours? And where are they?'

This was a good question. I said, 'I think they may have gone swimming.'

He didn't actually laugh, but the obvious lie and the presence of a cement mixer whose drum was still slowly revolving did seem comical, even to me.

'Let's see, shall we?' said he, springing up the steps to the alto terrazzo. I followed reluctantly, very much the condemned man en route to the gallows.

The fabulous view of the beach showed it to be deserted – no sign of any swimmers. But the carabiniere's eyes were sharper than mine, and he pointed to Gianni's dinghy, overturned on the sand by his ort.

I followed his finger, pointing apparently at nothing. Then he crooked it in a come hither gesture and a figure emerged from behind the dinghy – Pasquale.

I didn't know it – he didn't look it, but Pasquale was about to embark on his Finest Hour. Sheepish at first, he quickly resumed his old smiling swagger as he strolled towards us across the sand, smoking his usual cigarette. He greeted the officer confidently. I couldn't understand much of what they were saying, but I caught the words 'barca più grande'. Pasquale made gestures with his hands of something big, like the fish that got away.

'The padrone Inglese has a much bigger boat,' he meant, and, fortunately grasping the sheer genius of what he was suggesting, I rushed to the house, where a picture of the *Pedro*, my late lamented cabin cruiser, now under new ownership on the Norfolk Broads, painted by my daughter Mia, hung from a nail on the wall. To grab it and return with it to the terrace, where Pasquale and both officers were waiting, was the work of a moment. The carabinieri studied it with nods and smiles, and declared it a 'bellissima barca'. We all nodded and smiled. The whole thing made perfect sense. I needed a bigger boathouse because I had a bigger boat. Why a boat should need a bathroom was not mentioned.

We were all the best of friends as they left, with much backslapping and laughter and talk of meeting for a coffee some time soon in Brancaleone.

'Buon lavoro,' they said, as they drove away.

Dribs and drabs of the story were pieced together over the following days and weeks. Someone – a 'malo persona' – had denounced me to the Brancaleone carabinieri. The cops didn't like this person, but they had to act. Add the fact that I live in Palizzi, a different jurisdiction, and you get, with the genius of Pasquale, one very lucky Englishman. Those two carabinieri, with whom I have indeed had several coffees since, were only looking for a plausible reason to drop the case.

Nino soon reappeared, smiling and shaking his head, but Gianni wasn't seen again all day. He had run up into the mountains and hidden there for four hours before sneaking home under cover of darkness and hiding in his bedroom. Gianni 'Quattro Ora' became another one of our standing jokes.

11

Mad Dogs and Englishmen

The March weather was a definite improvement on February, bright sunshine interspersed with downpours and still chilly at night. For reasons unknown, it seemed to have a particularly virulent effect on the neighbourhood dogs.

The Calabrese relationship with their dogs is very different to that of the English – quite the opposite in fact. They are not kept as pets, but for practical purposes, like guarding and, in particular, hunting. The dogs live outside in cages, not inside on laps or cosy baskets. There is nothing suburban about Calabrese Man.

Just as coastal towns like Bova and Palizzi have mountain equivalents ('Marina' and 'Superiore'), so the Calabrese themselves, however marine they may have become, like Gianni, or upwardly mobile like Pino, retain the soul of the ancient mountain people they truly are. The montagnas tower behind them like Olympians, guarding and reminding, calling to their native sons to come up once more into the deep forests, where wolves still prowl in the primeval shadows, and wildcat, roe deer, otter, marten and the wild boar – the iconic cinghiale – roam as they did in medieval times, when the Normans came and added them to their bag. Falcon and eagle still wheel in the air as they always did, crying to the soul of Man the Hunter.

Somehow far more primitive than any American deer hunter is the sight of these blood-soaked Calabrese coming down from the mountain in their stained and faded battledress, their ferocious dogs foam-flecked from the hunt, the enormous, fearsome cinghiale roped to their cars. They are true hunter-gatherers, not just playing at it. The mountains are still meat and drink to them.

Pino and Gianni have vineyards in the mountains, small but big enough to provide a plentiful supply of wine, and in a garden shed a grape press and a good supply of wooden barrels. The wine, like the lethal limoncello, is fundamental to their way of life. Anyone who might have come among them, like me for instance, who had quit, or was trying to quit, drinking, might as well have arrived from the planet Zargon. The concept is unknown.

Pino was keen to induct me as deeply as possible into Calabrese ways. The Bova Marina Pig Festival was merely the shallow end of deeper mysteries. One day we set off to see 'a very simple person' he wanted me to meet, who lived in the mountains above Condofuri, and was, I suppose, the Calabrese equivalent of a huntsman from the English shires.

As a boy I used to hunt with the Chiddingfold Farmers, and I remember the awe in which I held Bob the Huntsman, who inhabited kennels rather than stables, home of the all-important hounds.

It was very different here, of course, but in many of the essentials, apart from the absence of horses, not. After much winding upwards we turned off a lane through some dry-stone gates, and the first thing to greet us was the baying of hounds. Brown and sleek – I suppose they were bloodhounds, or possibly the U Bucciriscu Calabrese hunting dog – six of them made enough noise for a couple of dozen English fox-hounds. They lived in a big wire enclosure some distance from the house, which we reached along a long stony track.

Simple he might have been, but his house was a dream. Built of stone into the mountainside, the rooms were white and cool, like monks' cells, with thick walls, and windows with rough wooden shutters – the very thing Bunty had been looking for.

Outside, cool wide verandas were shaded by thick bamboo, and we sat under one on white plastic chairs around a table laden with home-made cakes and bottles of generic and highly intoxicating liquors: stirrup cup without stirrups.

The huntsman's wife, who presided over all this hospitality, struck me as extremely versatile and charming, and it turned out that she supplemented whatever came in from her husband's hunting by running the local Agriturismo. This involved a kind of hostel, complete with bar and restaurant, which later we went to see, where eco-enthusiasts could stay and spend their daytimes trekking through the mountains, on or off donkeys, fishing, hiking, birdwatching, and eating food prepared by the huntsman's wife, home-made, locally caught or grown, like the feast she spread before us to welcome me.

Pino treated the very simple person with great respect, much as I would have done Bob, and though I couldn't understand the language, the guru-like asceticism of the hunter, the monastic purity of the rooms, the vaguely religious feeling surrounding the food and wine, emphasised the mystical nature of the hunt and the ancient legends buried in the landscape around us.

When I got home that night I dreamed of dogs, and I woke to them howling in the small hours. The cacophony was fantastic, but as usual there was one ringleader. The pattern was always the same: first the peace of the night would be disturbed by persistent, monotonous barking. Then the barks would escalate into howls; first one, then two, then every dog for miles around would join in, producing a bellowing disharmony, a symphony composed in hell.

I had identified the lead howler to the flats immediately across the road behind my house, an enclave of lawless and disreputable rustics surrounded by a collection of horses, goats, boats, chickens, pigs, unsilenced motorbikes and dogs – most of all, dogs. And among these dogs was the one I was after.

Normally I gave these neighbours a wide but friendly berth. Nobody in their right mind would want to fall out with them, least of all a foreigner.

But at three o'clock on this particular morning I was not in my right mind. I had had enough. Still wearing my pyjamas I got in my car and drove hell for leather the short distance along the lane, under the bridge, past the rubbish dump to the flats. I shone my headlights on the cages and there, sure enough, was the offending animal: a large, whitish, crossbred, evil-looking creature, somewhere between a Labrador and a husky and a god-knows-what. My shining lights did nothing to calm him – quite the opposite. His glowing eyes went from green to red and foam slavered from his teeth as he tried to rip the wire from his cage to get at me.

Even though I knew I'd crossed some kind of line, possibly from which there was no return, I blundered on, to shine my headlights on the flats themselves. Once in position I augmented my protest with long blasts on my horn. After a while a man in a red tank top came out onto one of the balconies, his hairy arms around the shoulders of two rumpled-looking women. I got out of the car and shouted 'Me no dormire, you no dormire' and shook my fist. Then I shook both fists and repeated myself.

Then I noticed he was laughing. He leaned over the balcony and called out, 'You are a crazy Inglese. I know who you are.' The women chorused, 'Crazy, crazy Inglese.' They were laughing too.

Suddenly I saw myself through their eyes and started laughing as well. Of course I was crazy, here in my pyjamas at three a.m. shouting my head off and waving my arms. I gave them a final, different sort of wave, a theatrical 'thank-you-and-goodnight' one, and goodbye, I hoped forever. Then I got in my car and drove home. The dogs were barking louder than ever.

Next morning I prepared my boiled eggs and coffee with a certain apprehension, not quite sure what to expect as an aftermath. He knew where I lived. It was hard to relax as I dunked my toast soldiers nervously into the yolks. Then Gianni and co. arrived and I felt safer.

In fact there was no aftermath. I saw him a few days later in his car. He gave me a small wave and a knowing smile, and on these nodding terms we remain. We understand each other. I am the crazy Inglese, and he lives his life exactly as he damn well pleases.

Not long after this I received word from Bunty, on my newly installed Telecom Italia telephone (courtesy of Gianni, who had a cousin who worked at the central exchange in Reggio), that she'd found a removals firm in Yorkshire willing to undertake the great trek with all our surplus goods from London to Spropoli. They were a small family firm, father and son, with one very large pantechnicon. They wanted to see a football match in Rome, and this was the sweetener needed to induce them. She had talked them down to 2,000 pounds, really a bargain for an eight-day, 7,000 kilometre round trip.

When the great day came it was raining cats and dogs. I got a call from a distressed-sounding Yorkshireman just after midday, to say they had reached Palizzi, were now lost, and had stopped in a lay-by somewhere.

The lorry would not be difficult to spot and I set off through the downpour in search of it.

Difficult to spot it certainly wasn't, and even in the rain a small crowd had gathered round the huge vehicle.

'You're almost there,' I said cheerfully.

'Where's all the sunshine?'

'Just follow me.'

We introduced ourselves properly when we got to the Bridge of the White Nightingale.

'There's no way she's going under there, mate,' said Simon, the father of the two.

'No way,' agreed Mark, the son.

To have come 3,000 miles and be stopped three hundred yards from home seemed pretty pathetic. The lane slopes steeply down into the riverbed under the road bridge, at an admittedly alarming angle for something as long and high as the Yorkshires' only business asset. Once stuck under there, I couldn't blame them for thinking that the lorry might never see home again.

Under the bridge and across the shallows from my lane is a fruit farm that large lorries regularly visit, which seem to get under okay, albeit with centimetres to spare. But when I told the Yorkshires this they shook their heads.

The lorry was stopped with its upper front almost touching the bridge. I didn't want to be the one responsible for causing a catastrophe, so I called Pasquale on the mobile phone. The idea was, I managed to explain, for him to come with Nino and his truck. We would unload onto that, bit by bit, in the pouring rain.

The Calabrese contingent duly arrived, and right away it was a standoff. Both pairs literally bristled with testosterone, but the Italians had the edge. Their contemptuous gesturing was too much for the reserved Yorkshiremen, and their knowledge of the terrain gave them the advantage. Without any interpretation needed they made it clear that the lorry would get under the bridge easily, given sufficient skill and nerve.

The gauntlet having been thrown down, the Yorkshires climbed into their cab with grim determination, concern for their lorry superseded by National Pride, plus the natural taciturnity of Yorkshire folk.

The stage was set. Pasquale and Nino took up position under the bridge, guiding the huge vehicle into the abyss of shifting gravel and deep shadow. I held my breath as the roof of the lorry inched agonisingly under, so close to the ironwork as to seem that jam fast it must.

But it didn't. Miraculously, and with nothing to spare, it passed beneath and was level once more.

Nino and Pasquale shook their heads. Any triumph the Yorkshires might have felt was gently ridiculed. 'Gli Inglesi non sono bravi,' I heard them mutter. 'Niente cojones.'

The Yorkshires swung the lorry left into the lane with alarming violence, so it rocked to and fro as it set off down the narrow rutted route to journey's end.

It came to an equally alarming halt at the sharp right-hander into the Buntessa gates. By the time we caught up with them they were shaking their heads again.

By now there was no impossibility Nino and Pasquale weren't prepared to challenge them into. But there was a ninety-degree turn, with no room whatever to manoever a fifty-foot truck.

Ahead was the old ruined house, and to the left the railway track. Between the railway and the lane is a bank, picturesquely overgrown with cactus and prickly pear.

It was up this bank the Calabrese were proposing the Yorkshires should, by a series of miniscule turns, gradually shift the back end round so the front end pointed at the gates.

So intense had the rivalry become between the nations that Simon and Mark, two generations of experience, actually began to force the back wheels of their precious breadwinner up the bank of the unfenced Seaside Line.

First it stuck fast. Then, after much revving, it suddenly leapt backwards and landed on the tracks. The lorry was straddling the line. All it needed now for the disaster to be complete was a train. Even Nino and Pasquale looked worried.

The tyres kept spinning on the smooth metal of the rail. Then suddenly they gripped, the lorry bounded into the air, seemed to hang suspended, then slid down the bank and back onto the lane with a tremendous, sickening judder. Its position in relation to the Villa La Buntessa was unchanged.

Now began the long slow humiliating retreat, reversing back along the lane, until the lorry was back under the bridge, where unloading could begin onto Nino's truck in relative dryness.

The side doors were opened to reveal the accumulation of decades; beloved junk that would transform our beach house into a home.

To the average Italian, Nino and Pasquale included, such rubbish should have been left on the dump before the bridge. Their body language clearly indicated that bringing it all this way was the strongest evidence yet of the perversity of Inglesis, and that asking them to participate was little short of an insult.

Shabby cupboards and old dressers, tired-looking beds and bunks, boxes of books, armchairs with stuffing and springs sticking out, bikes and trikes with missing spokes, boxes of old toys, a rickety ping-pong table, an even ricketier gypsy cart packed with buckets and spades and other beach paraphernalia, an ancient typewriter, innumerable boxes of kitchen utensils, carton upon carton of sheets, towels, pillows, duvets and blankets; some painted wooden book-shelves, a rocking horse without a tail, a large mahogany glass-fronted bookcase, stacks of wooden chairs in various states of disrepair, piles of pictures and paintings tied together with string, a drum kit, several guitars, an amp (extremely heavy), a new Ikea L-shaped sofa, a pine kitchen table and chairs, a large leather-topped desk, a large antique mirror in a wooden frame wrapped in cardboard and two more mirrors similarly wrapped.

The whole heavy, ungainly jumble was disembowelled from the dark interior and lowered, load by seemingly interminable load, onto Nino's flatbed truck.

Down the lane they went. Stair-rods of rain attacked the teetering piles as Nino's truck juddered and bumped its way to journey's end. Some things got a much-needed wash, others a soaking that mould-ered cardboard and sank damply into tattered upholstery.

I supervised distribution between the house, soon at least no longer bleak, the barakka, where there was room for a considerable overflow, and the garage, where things which frankly didn't seem of much use, at least for the moment, could be stored.

While the Yorkshires did the loading it was Nino and Pasquale who helped me unload, with the result that each item was minutely scruti-nised before reaching its final resting place. Every rickety chair and bent bicycle was given the Italian once-over. It was all most embarrassing.

The difference in taste between the declining English classes, posh-but-poor and brought up on Winnie-the-Pooh, and upwardly inclined southern Italians, who like to see a shine on everything, is a cultural divide that can never be crossed and is pointless trying to explain. I therefore stuck to shrugging, and smiling inscrutably at their unspoken questions and mounting disbelief as the eccentric details of our consignment were revealed.

As dusk fell the rain diminished and the work was done. By now Calabrese and Inglesi were grandi amici, and Nino and Pasquale drove off waving.

Simon and Mark said they wanted a 'sarnie', but the nearest equivalent, a panini, I knew couldn't be found. All the bread runs out at mezzogiorno.

So I offered to cook, and to my dismay they accepted. Leaving the lorry under the bridge, we repaired to the barakka and Tralongo's ancient stove, where I concocted a combination of pasta and fish fingers, all that I had. After a hard day it wasn't much, but at least there was lots of it. I asked them to stay and have a refreshing swim in the morning, but the rainy beach and the fact there were no beds without unearthing them from the damp morass they'd just jettisoned I think put them off.

Late as it was, we backed the mighty pantechnicon up the slope and round the rubbish dump until it pointed back towards Brancaleone, where I said they would find somewhere to stay.

Subsequent enquiries at the San Giorgio drew a blank, so I never learned what became of them. I think they just wanted to get the hell out of Calabria.

Pino came by a few days later, ostensibly to invite me to dinner, but I knew really to take a gander at the tatty furniture, word about which had spread far and wide. He looked a bit shocked, before taking a safe seat on the rock-like surface of the brand-new orange divano.

'Soon there will be a very simple meal,' he announced, for all the men of his boar-hunting gang. The guests of honour were to be myself and the Very Simple Person.

12

Going Fast Slowly

As April moved towards May and Bunty's next visit, I began to think that progress, which until now had often seemed uncomfortably like careering downhill in an out-of-control handcart, was in fact not really going anywhere. 'Going fast slowly', Pino called it: lots of activity, lots of bills, yet nothing you could put your finger on that brought us significantly closer to housing over twenty people in August, suddenly only weeks away.

It was therefore a relief to hear from Domenico, who I'd almost forgotten about, that the wooden house had arrived in the port of Vibo Valentia, and that he would soon be going down there to sort out the documents.

Anything arriving from Romania is automatically regarded with suspicion by Italian officialdom, so it was some time before Domenico triumphantly announced the imminent arrival of a 'grande camion', bringing the long-awaited casa di legno.

Pasquale, Nino, Gianni and I were waiting by the rubbish tip at the appointed hour, keeping a sharp lookout. But the thing that hove into view two hours late, which we knew could only be it, was so enormous you could have fitted four of the Yorkshires' removal van into it with room to spare. Any question of it getting under the Bridge of the White Nightingale, or anywhere near the helipad, had to be immediately ruled out, and a Plan B improvised on the hoof.

Plan B was Gianni's cousin Nino. His builder's yard in Palizzi would become the staging post, and his truck commandeered to supplement our Nino's truck (there are a lot of Ninos in Italy!) in the ultimate transportation of the wooden house.

Anyone in Palizzi who didn't already know about my wooden house soon did. The whole town was not only talking about it, many became actively involved, because Nino's yard is at the very top of the town, reached by a series of narrow streets with sharp bends in them, all of which had to be delicately negotiated. Anyone who didn't actually live on the route had at least one relative who did. Nobody wanted to be left out of the business of advising the driver which way to turn, or of finding the person whose gate had to be opened to allow the monster that fraction more space that might make all the difference, or of advising their neighbour that their balcony was about to be wiped out. Nothing much happens in Palizzi, and this had all the hallmarks of becoming a Big Day.

The yard itself is up a steep ramp, round a sharp bend beside a block of flats. The ramp was a bridge too far for the monster, so the bend by the flats became its stopping point, blocking the road; anyone who wanted to get past had to go round. In England this would have led to mayhem and furious remonstrations. Here in Palizzi the opposite was the case. Anyone who found their way blocked merely became curious to know what interesting thing might be happening and how they could involve themselves in some capacity or other, rather than the humdrum business of continuing on their journey.

All the bits of the house had to be sweated up the ramp manually before being sorted onto the trucks, and there really was a lot of it. They say many hands make light work, and in this case it was true. Everyone wanted to be able to tell their grandchildren they'd carried a bit.

When it was all piled up, and Nino's yard pretty well impassable, all hands and minds returned to the monster truck and how to extricate it backwards. Once that was done it was mezzogiorno and everybody vanished.

Nothing else happened till next morning, when Domenico himself made an appearance. I was drinking my coffee, staring out to sea, watching the little fishing boats landing their morning catch, when down the drive his BMW came roaring. It was all very Non Tranquillo.

His blue business suit shone incongruously as ever in the morning sun, and his greeting was as irritatingly breezy as usual, considering how hopelessly behind schedule the whole thing was and what a hoohah yesterday had been for everyone except him.

'Buongiorno.' Of course I had to be friendly and pretend to be pleased to see him, since I was still pretty well completely in his power. All I had so far was a 7,000 euro pile of wood.

'Where is the house?' said Domenico.

'You might well ask.'

Soon the first two truckloads arrived, and he was able to transfer his annoying behaviour to Nino and Pasquale, bossing them around with his usual lack of tact. Gradually the different bits were sorted out and arranged around the site in order of priority, ready for Domenico's team of Romanian 'operai', whose expertise he assured us guaranteed the finished house in less than ten days. All that remained was for him to let us know when Day One was.

It wasn't until mid-May, a week before Bunty, that the Romanians finally arrived. At least it would nearly be done, I thought, with the helipad obscured and vindicated. I greeted them with enthusiasm, unlike the Calabrese, who disappeared into the boathouse and pretended to be too busy to have anything to do with them.

There were five of them plus Domenico, and my enthusiasm took a knock when he told me they'd be living-in for the duration, him included. They would commandeer the barakka. He had it all worked out.

'But—!' I was speechless.

The barakka has a bathroom and kitchen, he pointed out, and the men have sleeping bags. They were used to living rough, much rougher than this; and then there was the sea! If they needed a wash they could leap into the Ionian, which is what they all immediately did.

The Calabrese watched their antics from the boathouse with pursed lips. It was all very non bravo. But what could you expect from such people?

If I'd been wondering what exactly I'd stored in the barakka the Romanians soon opened my eyes. The whole consignment might have been put there for their convenience. They delved into boxes and stripped off packing paper, until it was a regular home-from-home. Plates, cups, pots, pans, blankets, trestle tables, jugs, glasses – by the time they got to the bottom of it they lacked for nothing. The following evening they invited me for dinner.

Domenico ushered me to my chair with only slightly exaggerated ceremony. The wine was flowing, the atmosphere merry, and my feeling of weirdness soon wore off. Looking at the familiar objects of a lifetime become the casual utilities of Romanian strangers was surreal, but at least they were Getting On With It. It was no different, I supposed, to having an army billeted on you, or living in an occupied country.

They certainly knew how to cook, and Tralongo's ancient stove was stretched to providing a five-course feast without apparent difficulty. It was oddly reassuring that the barakka could become a happy home for so many people, full of warmth and laughter. They told me they never wanted to leave.

But leave they did, the very next day. Domenico said there was an emergency at another job and they would only be gone for twenty-four hours. But I never saw them again. They never came back.

Disaster though this was, Gianni and co. were delighted. Not that they weren't sympathetic to my plight; they just gloried in the confirmation of their darkest prejudices against Romanians, Albanians, people from the Balkans generally, and, with the possible exception of myself, anyone who wasn't Calabrese (excluding Domenico, now Public Enemy Number One).

We stood there perusing the dereliction that so recently had been progress. The sides were up, and a few roof beams, but that was it. The rest was piled up any old how, exposed to the weather, and to the eyes that I knew would not be blind forever.

Bunty arrived on the Sunday. We got out of the car by the gates and patrolled what I'd been telling her about en route from the airport, trying my best to break it gently. It was all very dreadful, but the May weather was glorious, in vivid contrast to her last trip. The goods had arrived, the boathouse, though not finished, was at least 'up', and hope springs eternal, especially in sunshine.

'Pasquale says he can find some men to finish the wooden house,' I assured her. 'He'll be here tomorrow.'

But tomorrow came and Pasquale didn't. Nor did Gianni, nor Nino, nor anybody. At first we thought perhaps they'd tactfully left us to ourselves for romantic reasons, but the following day the place was deserted as ever, and the sense of emptiness began to get to us. A strong breeze from the sea blew cement dust across the abandoned works in a most depressing manner.

That evening we went up to Gianni's house to make enquiries. His wife Enza invited us in for coffee – a lengthy ritual that cannot be refused. We congregated in the small kitchen, while the rest of Gianni's family, minus the man himself, was rounded up to join in the occasion. There's no such thing as a quick drop-in in southern Italy.

The fact that Bunty was with me only added to the greatness of the occasion. Gianni's father, who is extremely old and speaks a dialecto which no one, not just me, seems able to understand, was rooted out from his vegetable patch in their large farm-like garden, where goats and pigs and chickens graze under the olive trees. He shook hands and, smiling and nodding, sat down on his chair at the kitchen table. Gianni's mother, who may be even older, and whose mind took a wrong turn some years back, sat in front of her bowl of baby food and was fed pills from a colourful assortment by Enza's sister. Gianni's huge and always smiling brother Nino, whose mind had wandered at birth, completed the party.

Bunty spoke to them all slowly in heavily accented English, her invariable procedure with foreigners, which they seemed to enjoy, if not entirely understand, judging by the nods and smiles around the table. The coffee came and with it, presented ceremonially on paper doilies, were little cakes that crumbled onto the table when we ate them.

'Non ti preoccupare,' Enza exclaimed in horror when Bunty tried to brush up the crumbs. 'Tranquillo, Bunty.'

Gradually we worked the conversation round, language barrier by language barrier, to the possible whereabouts of Gianni and the others.

They had decided to take a short holiday, a week or so, perhaps ten days, in Trento, where Gianni's sister lived, close to the Austrian border.

Why they had chosen this moment and never mentioned it, at least to me, remained a mystery. Enza spread her arms expressively, palms upwards, in the small kitchen. Who could explain the ways of men?

It was as good a way as any of looking at it. Who could explain so many things around here? It was useless to try, and I encouraged Bunty to relax and enjoy the sunshine. They would soon return, 'Speriamo'.

We sat on the beach and ventured gingerly into the shallows. It was still pretty chilly, though some hardy types were swimming further along. Probably their warm southern blood was more accustomed.

Afternoons were spent this way, but in the mornings Bunty wanted to get on with things. Whereas I tend to sit and stare out to sea, or read a book from the piles now available, she didn't think that the absence of the men meant downing tools ourselves. She is an indefatigable sort of person, obsessed with finding things to do, quite the opposite to me, master of the art of doing nothing.

One dreadful morning she entered the boathouse with a measuring tape and very soon all hell broke loose. Not only had I not built the simple cottage she'd specified (or not specified, depending on your point of view), but I hadn't measured what I had built, so the bed wouldn't fit where she wanted it.

'You just didn't think.'

'I didn't think you wanted it there. I thought you'd want it facing out to sea.'

'That *would've* been nice, if you hadn't covered over the terrace.'

This was the main bone of contention, round which the whole issue pivoted. Irrespective of the roof terrace with its recently added balustrada, which did admittedly add an even greater sense of grandiosity, there was the question of the more modest lower terrace, that would have looked out to sea, had the simple cottage plan been stuck to, and had that terrace not been covered by a roof, with sloping wooden beams, creating what Pasquale called the 'Grande Salone'.

The sea could now be viewed through a huge expensive picture window. The little terrace, so brutishly abandoned, would have had a lovely indoor/outdoor kitchen, complete with pizza oven.

'But what you don't realise,' I said, for once in the right, 'is that it was architecturally impossible. You couldn't weatherproof windows or a wall or anything where you wanted the bedroom to end, and you couldn't cover the terrace in bamboo because the first winter storm would blow it all away.'

She didn't believe me and she still doesn't.

'And what's going to go where the bed won't fit?' she demanded. 'You hadn't thought of that, had you?'

I hadn't. Under the huge window, which not just Bunty thought at least one too many, it looked like there was a huge gap.

'How about a sofa – a sort of window seat?'

'What would you look at? The side of the bed?'

I hadn't thought it through. I'd never built a house before.

'You try arguing with Pasquale,' I said.

That's when she had her Brilliant Idea. She hurried to the house and rummaged in her bag, coming up shortly with an Italian magazine she'd bought at Rome airport. Racing through the pages she found what she was looking for: a terracotta-coloured cement bathtub, complete with directions in Italian to create one in your own home.

When the men finally returned the following week she showed it to them. Gianni and Pasquale snorted and gesticulated, then walked away flapping their hands. But Nino looked thoughtful, and took the magazine home to study it.

Next morning his truck rumbled down the drive with an old bathtub roped on the back. Using a bathtub as a mould wasn't in the directions, but Nino has his own way of doing things. He carried the bathtub into the boathouse and very soon his yellow cement mixer was rumbling away. Bunty and he had a series of conferences, and by that evening the cement bathtub was in place and the old one back on Nino's truck.

We stood and admired it – even Gianni and Pasquale. It wasn't terracotta yet – that needed a special non-porous cement coating mixed with oxblood substitute – but the gap in the bedroom had been filled in spectacular fashion, and in the 'instant' way that Bunty could taste the intoxicating exhilaration of for herself.

Next on her agenda was the Blue Terrace. On one of the mornings of their absence, when she wasn't knee-deep in homemaking, she'd found some beautiful blue tiles in Brancaleone, to match a terrace we'd seen in *Seaside Style*, our bible of ideas for beach living. Though the inspiration was Italian, in the nearby Aeolian Islands, it failed to inspire Gianni and co. They were dubious. Terraces were red, not blue.

Nevertheless the Maestro di Matonelli was summoned. His would be the final word. Without him the tiles could not be laid.

He arrived, burly and grizzly and much deferred to, with his assistente.

The assistente did all the talking, while the maestro stood majestically by, surveying the area between the boathouse and the barakka in a godlike manner. It had been levelled with about a million tons of cement and was ready to receive tiles whenever we were.

The idea of the blue was they would stand out against the surrounding white, giving the false impression of a swimming pool shimmering against the backdrop of the sea and sky.

The maestro examined Bunty's sample of blue tile like a high priest before a sacrifice. The laying of tiles in Italy is an art that pre-dates Etruscan times, and cannot be taken lightly. When laid they glow and the whole becomes far greater than the sum of its parts. The maestro sniffed the tile and rubbed it with his finger.

It was a great relief all round when finally he smiled, nodded his emperor-like head and pronounced the tile 'bellissima'.

Even the sceptics laughed and said, 'Bravo'. Hands were shaken, and the maestro kissed Bunty on both cheeks.

Now began the great process of laying the Blue Terrace. It became a tourist attraction from the start. Friends and relations of all parties even remotely concerned came to see for themselves whether what they'd heard could be really true. Small and large groups appeared in the drive at all hours, but evenings were worst. In the end Bunty and I took to going out and leaving them to it. The strain of explanation and congratulation was too wearing when repeated innumerable times. We explored the gelaterias and cafés of the surrounding towns until we thought the coast might be clear again at home.

One evening we went as far as Bovalino (reputedly 'Paese di Paul Getty', built on the proceeds of his kidnapping), where the giant Euro-Spar drew Bunty like a magnet. Housed in a mall the like of which we never expected to see on our undiscovered coast, it was a treat for an urban habituée of London and Los Angeles like her. I trailed behind her as she scoured it from end to end. No stone was left unturned. Among other delights she found a lightweight wheel-barrow, which we managed to force into the back of the Clio. Now we could do some proper gardening, she said, as opposed to my tree-buying extravaganzas. When we got back she locked it in the garage: 'So "they" can't get at it.'

'But "they" have a key,' I said. 'They store their stuff there when they're working on the wooden house.'

Which they weren't, of course – nobody was.

The Blue Terrace progressed and one day an enormous pile of sand arrived – really a mountain – delivered by Nino di Palizzi and dumped onto the drive. It seemed an awful lot more than we could possibly need and I couldn't help noticing the consignment of bricks he also had on board, which he left outside Gianni's ort.

Sure enough, that evening Gianni appeared, wheeling Bunty's new barrow. 'All this sand blocking the drive,' he explained, was 'bruto', and could cause us a 'grande problema'. It was 'troppo', but we needn't worry. He would remove the excess and get rid of it.

He then proceeded, load by load, to shovel most of our sand into the barrow and wheel it round to his ort.

Bunty was understandably outraged. 'We have to pay for that sand! How much did it cost? How much is the terrace costing?'

But I just shook my head. After five months I was an old hand at this. These were questions that could never be answered.

'That's not the way it works,' I said.

'Then how *does* it work?'

'It works the way you just saw, with Gianni and the sand. Nino is his cousin, I am the padrone. It's been the custom in southern Italy since time immemorial: the padrone must be cheated and pretend not to notice. It's just a game really, and without it life wouldn't be the same.'

She shook her head. 'I thought they were our friends.'

'Oh, they're our friends all right. If they didn't like us we wouldn't be here. We wouldn't last five minutes.'

13

The Devil in the Garden

The Mystery of the Disappearing Romanians became clearer in June. Apparently the emergency at the other site had escalated when one of them fell off the roof and broke his neck. This had alerted the emergency services, including the police. Examination of documents quickly revealed the Romanians not to have work permits, and they were deported forthwith. Domenico's whole operation was now under investigation.

Pasquale and co. did not attempt to conceal their delight. When I pointed out that I was left with a 7,000 euro pile of wood they said, 'Tranquillo, Ian. Non ti preoccupare.'

The gist of the arithmetic, according to Pasquale, meant that I might easily be quids in. If the total cost was 15,000 euros he would see to it that whoever he found to replace the Romanians would keep me well in the black.

'Y quando?' I asked. When would this miracle worker be found? August was just around the corner, and Bunty said the family were definitely all coming en masse. The situation was getting desperate.

Pasquale shrugged expressively. Who could say when the fates might smile on us, especially with the heat of summer making work even less attractive than usual.

Meanwhile the Blue Terrace was finished, and the June sun blazed on its shimmering surface. The terrace tourism increased, with Pino often in the role of guide to 'some very important people'. What we hadn't realised was that the blue combined with the surrounding white were the colours of Greece, and here in the heart of

Magna Graecia we were seen to have made an important symbolic statement.

One sunny day Pino came strolling down the drive with his latest very important person. The visitor wore a blue cotton safari shirt and his hair was swept back from his forehead in a 1940s sort of style, exactly like my father. His ears, nose and mouth, and in particular his diabolic smile bore the same uncanny resemblance to someone who had always made me feel about three inches tall. It was all what Jeeves would have called 'most disturbing'.

This was my next-door neighbour, the professore. 'Luciano', as he insisted I call him (could that be Italian for Lucifer?) put his arm around my shoulder in a show of extreme bonhomie.

He admired the works and bowed to Bunty, whose hand he gallantly kissed, all of which I found thoroughly alarming. Then he cross-examined me about my books: could he get them in Italian? Which was the one about Ancient Greece? What were the ISBN numbers? Not only was he just like my father, he was beginning to sound like my old headmaster as well.

As for Ancient Greece, I don't know where he got that from, but Pino was the obvious suspect. He had a way of talking me up which I thought could only be helpful, so long as it was never put to the test. I heard him tell one group of terrace tourists that I 'had written many famous films'. Rather than a mere 'scrittore' I became the 'Grande Scrittore Inglese', a title I secretly basked in.

Now the professore's ostensibly polite enquiries seemed bent on unmasking me. The general unease I felt about him escalated into the guilty misery of an ink-stained schoolboy discovered in some loathsome deceit. When he asked for the ISBN numbers I knew the game was up. I said I'd let him know, hoping he'd never mention them again, which he never has.

I was so busy being intimidated that I failed to be as suspicious as I should have been at this sudden show of cameraderie from a person who was obviously, even to my diminished powers of observation, only self-interested. He didn't give two hoots about me or my books. He was up to something.

I got my first inkling of what this something was about two weeks later, after Bunty had gone. At first the true horror of the thing didn't register. I saw Luciano over the fence, standing on his roof, waved at him, and got on with my day.

I didn't give it another thought until later, when he was up there again, this time with another man. They were walking about in an inspecting sort of way, and this time I assumed it must be something to do with roofing.

Next day they were up there again, this time with a tall pole, which they erected in the middle of the roof. Only when it was up did I notice the length of twine, which each of them took an end of, to either side of the roof, making a huge triangle.

That's when the penny dropped. I didn't want to believe it, and for some time I told myself that such a thing couldn't really be happening. But in the end I had to face it: he was building another storey on his house, one which would not only overlook me, but loom over me like a colossus. All my work, all my money, everything I had done and dreamed of, were suddenly under threat. And from a man who looked exactly like my father. Could he possibly be reaching from the grave to thwart me yet again?

And who had known about this? Who could possibly *not* have known?

Pino was at his beach house and I drove round there in a rage. The idea that I'd been set up, that Tralongo had pulled a fast one on me with Pino's connivance, brought me dangerously close to forgetting the niceties of behaviour needed when one person in southern Italy calls upon another at their house.

I fumed inwardly as I said, 'Permesso?' at the gate.

'Ian.' The whole family was there, unmistakably thrilled to see me. As I kissed Celeste's soft smiling cheeks I reflected that this was a person incapable of harming another. Anyway it was I, wasn't it, who had arrived here out of the blue? No one had sought me out.

I looked around the familiar terrace. The whole thing was my idea from the start.

On the other hand, no one had warned me. Innocent though Celeste and the children must undoubtedly be, what about Pino? Nothing went on around here that he didn't know about.

I turned to him, ready to remonstrate, but even as I did so a warning voice spoke in my ear. Whether he knew or not is something I will never know. But if I ever need help, which I undoubtedly will, Pino is the only person I can turn to. He is my protector, my godfatherly consigliere. Offend him and I'm definitely doomed. The doom of the professore's monstrosity was only probable.

'Per favore,' I said, sitting down and shaking my head, so they could see something was up.

'Problemi?' said Viviana, looking unbearably sympathetic.

'Si. Grandi problemi.'

If the explanation that followed was to be believed – and I wanted to believe it – they were just as surprised as I was, and just as horrified. Looking at it from their house, the new storey would loom over them almost as much as over me.

But what could you do? The professore was an unstoppable force, a law unto himself, the self-appointed dittatore of our little community, who didn't care about anybody, whose brother was a judge in Reggio, and some of whose friends were 'brute persone'. He must have got permission from the mayor of Reggio, over-ruling or otherwise strong-arming the Comune di Palizzi.

Nevertheless we could speak to him. Pino would come with me. We couldn't stop him building it, but maybe something could be done to ameliorate the impact. No overlooking windows, for example.

The professore was friendlier than ever when we arrived. He could imagine nothing more horrible than upsetting his new friend and neighbour the Inglese. But what could he do, short of not building it, which he had every right to, and permission for, granted over two years ago? It was the regulation five metres back from the fence, and as for windows, there was the morning sun to the east to be considered, not just views of sea and mountains as we suggested.

But he would think about it. Yes, he would certainly think about it. Meanwhile the works, which were to begin imminently, would of course be carried out with the minimum of disturbance.

I hadn't imagined they'd be starting *now*, just when the family were arriving. Nobody here began building in the height of summer – it was unheard of. By the time we left, things seemed worse than ever. Warm words, but the message was clear: I was well and truly f****d.

Possibly because he thought it might cheer me up, soon after this Pino announced the much-vaunted Cinghiale Hunt Lunch. He held it at his beach house, where he had impressive outdoor cooking facilities, including a barbecue and pizza oven over which he presided. As is usual, the less spectacular cooking was done indoors by the womenfolk, with Celeste in charge of a small army of female friends and relatives from Galati, where both she and Gianni grew up.

Another small army of frankly tough-looking Calabrese hardmen arrived in a variety of battered-looking cars, mostly 4×4 Pandas, favoured locally for their cheapness and mountaineering capabilities.

I felt marginally less of a middle-class ponce, in this company of hunters of an animal whom most of them closely resembled, because I was with Gianni. We arrived together and I made a great show of what grandi amici we were, our arms around each other's shoulders in a rough, manly sort of way.

The biggest problem was always going to be the drinking. Ever since I'd arrived in Calabria I'd had to compromise and generally keep quiet about the fact that I'd quit. It was no good trying to explain to the likes of Pino, even though he is a doctor, that a lifetime of excess had led at last to the Palace of Wisdom, whereby a person looks back on all the cock-ups he's made, and realises that in almost every case it was drink-related. Furthermore, my system had packed up under the strain and the hangovers were kicking in immediately after the first glass. The game was no longer worth the candle.

The fact that we now live in a touchy-feely world only made things worse in company such as this, where group hugging and recitation of the Serenity Prayer are unlikely ever to catch on. These guys hug wild boar and wrestle them to the ground. They drink until they drop, and if that means dead, so be it.

Gianni, I knew, was working later that afternoon, driving his bus in Reggio. He couldn't drink either, and I was hoping that two refuseniks sitting together might distract attention from one of them.

The Very Simple Person arrived and the beano was on. There was an immediate upending of bottles into tall plastic tumblers. Someone had made Vino Greca in his vineyard and the general idea was to test it by drinking as much of it as possible. No wine-tasting and spitting-out nonsense here.

Someone upended a bottle into my tumbler until it was full. I tried to ignore it, noticing too late that Gianni had cunningly filled his own with Coke.

I got away with sipping and smiling only for the length of time it took for polite deference to my status as a scrittore Inglese, friend of Pino and person of reputed great wealth (Gianni insisted on referring to me as Mister Spendi Spendi) to wear off – approximately the first couple of courses and bottles per person.

The food was delicious and the women attentive, and I honestly thought I was going to get away with it, until someone upended a wine bottle into Gianni's glass of Coke. The unwelcome attention of the hunters had turned to us, led by Pino, who was making aggressive 'What The Right Arm's For' gestures in our direction.

In the film *Conduct Unbecoming* a group of British officers of an Indian regiment in the days of the Raj engage in an after-dinner amusement called Pig Sticking. This involves hunting down some unfortunate person, usually an Indian, but on one notorious occasion an officer's widow, with sharpened sticks and view-halloos. I don't know if you've seen it, but it flashed through my mind at this moment. Visions of myself becoming quarry, and of being hunted down and pig-stuck among the prickly pears, suddenly seemed only too likely if I went on making even more of an outsider of myself than I already was.

Like Gianni therefore I drained the bitter cup, which after a couple of refills wasn't so bitter after all. Pino was pleased. Honour was satisfied. He said to me, 'It is better to live like a lion for one day than like a lamb for your whole life.'

The bitterness came later, complete with pounding head and nauseous despairing thoughts, but at least I could lie down and listen to the sea. I pitied poor old Gianni in his boiling bus.

In late July work began in earnest on the professore's house, just days before the arrival of my famiglia. This was a bitterness that could not so easily be remedied. Could I build a fifty-foot high wall? Plant some kind of instant forest? My mind seethed with ideas of reparation and revenge, but nothing like a solution. Meanwhile my own building works had ground to a virtual halt. The boathouse was at least finished, but the wooden house remained stalled.

'How come he can get people to work in Luglio and Agosto but not me?' I asked Pasquale, with some bitterness.

'Because he is the professore.'

Next day he and Nino began a token display of working on the wooden house, in the absence of replacement operai. They exchanged slightly reserved banter with the professore's army of workers, who from their vantage point on the roof had a bird's-eye view of everything we were doing. His new storey was going up fast, and the higher it went the more it would loom over what was rapidly becoming our Paradise Lost.

Then, two days later, the carabinieri arrived. They pulled up in the drive, yards from where Pasquale and Nino were working. This time the game was surely up, and could only be the result of a denunciation from Luciano's roof spies. It was the final straw for me, and I was ready to march round there and commit violence, or at least unleash the cri de coeur I'd never had the nerve to vent against my father.

I watched in fascinated horror as two (a different two) carabinieri got out of their car and walked over to where Nino and Pasquale were standing, building tools in hand, like frozen statues of 'Calabrese Man'. They were banged to rights and no mistake – we all were.

But then, miracle of miracles, the thing became a re-run of the last bust. There was no mistaking the bonhomie that followed the brief conversation, the backslapping, shoulder-holding, handshaking chumminess, as Pasquale and Nino escorted the officers back to their vehicle.

'Buon lavoro,' they called, and were gone, backing out into the lane with a final farewell toot.

'What the hell?' I said it in English but my meaning was clear. Nino and Pasquale were clapping their hands and rolling around. They grabbed me in a delirious embrace as they tried to get the words out. They'd got the wrong house! They'd come to bust the professore!

This was just too marvellous to believe. Sweet revenges like this don't happen. We waited with bated breath for the blow to fall. Sure enough, twenty minutes later all work next door ceased. The drills and cement mixers fell silent. The men disappeared from the roof. The professore's building project had been closed down.

But it was too good to be true and I knew it. I wanted to believe it desperately, that the threat to my happiness had been averted and the devil in my garden seen off.

But Lucifer, having fallen, has a nasty habit of rising again, and sure enough, two days later all the hellish banging and hammering and drilling was back again, rending the tranquil air and dashing my hopes of salvation.

And all this two days before Bunty was due to arrive to make the place welcoming for the family.

14

My Family and Other

When Bunty and I got married in the sixties it was for keeps, for better or worse. Her family was grand and poor – or at least 'cash' poor – mine suburban and rich, or at least seemed rich, to go by the trappings. A match made in heaven you might say. Anyway we were in love, and we both wanted a large family, which we set about producing with the frenzied sexual energy of parents barely out of their teens. By the time she was twenty-five Bunty had four kids, with two more in the offing. The question of money, though by then permanently critical, didn't stop us.

Homes came and went. We moved to California and back. I worked as a radio pirate, in the rag trade, the music business, as Flipper (my nickname) the Hollywood rollerskating nightclub host, as a Beverly Hills butler, screen hack and novelist.

None of which made me rich, and all of which presumably had its impact on the children. It wasn't normal, but then again it wasn't ordinary. It taught them to stand on their own feet, in the case of the boys onstage in rock bands, of our daughters Holly and Mia in film production, and of Liberty on the catwalk. The entertainment industry claimed them all in their formative Los Angeles years. The idea that it's better to be up there doing it, win or lose, than down there in the crowd, safe and sorry, infected the whole family, and took the place of good, sensible parenting. They saw too much 1980s glitz and sham Spandex glamour when they were kids to ever want to live in a world of suits and nine-to-five.

Now they were all arriving, the whole motley crew, complete with partners and kids, more like a migration than a holiday. Alitalia gave us a group discount.

Bunty arrived a few days ahead of time, to get things ready and make sure the welcome would be as good as it could be, which, when the full catastrophe became clear, she realised might not be all that good – the place was little short of a disaster zone.

But at least it would be a warm one. That summer was the hottest on record in the Mediterranean for years, with temperatures soaring into the forties and whole countries catching fire.

I kept seeking reassurance from Gianni and co. Was this 'normale', or 'non normale'? Was this one more thing I'd overlooked, one more nail in the coffin? If it got so hot you couldn't live here, maybe that accounted for me being the only Inglese in town. Adding global warming into the equation, would what I'd bought soon be uninhabitable?

Their replies varied according to the number of forest fires actively in progress in the hills behind us. Sometimes it struck them as non normale to see quite that much smoke blotting out the blue of the sky, quite that many big yellow planes scooping up water from the sea and dumping it on the flames.

One load landed on Gianni's ort – definitely non normale, not to mention ruinous for his tomatoes.

'Surely it's a heat wave,' I said, 'a *heat wave*?'

But he just shook his head, and went off to hose the salt off his vegetables with water from my well.

Bunty got busy making the best of things, and I told her how happy the Romanians, responsible though they were for our present difficulties, had been in the barakka.

The barakka has shantytown charm, and I'd installed a ceiling fan that stirred the air lazily, like something in a Somerset Maugham story. But whether, in all this heat, it was really habitable by northern Europeans with children was something we weren't sure about at all. And suspicious droppings kept appearing, the calling cards of lizards, or possibly something worse. They say you're never more than six feet from a rat, and in the barakka this figure can probably be narrowed down considerably. Strange scratching and scrabbling noises often startled me when sitting there at my mother's desk, which I'd installed by the window. Staring out to sea and musing, chewing my pencil with a view to writing, my tranquil thoughts had been disturbed more than once by fleeting shadows, real or imagined, scuttling along wainscots, furtive and furry and ferocious when cornered.

In the end we decided to sleep in the barakka ourselves. It was the only answer. If anyone was going to have their throats torn out by vermin it would have to be us. One other person could brave it with us on the single bed – probably Leo, the only remaining single of our tribe. The others would have to pack into the villa somehow, and the boathouse, which did at least have a bath in the bedroom, if only one loo in the bathroom.

'Thank goodness for the Grande Salone,' I said, vindicated at least for the moment. It was grande enough to sleep five.

We drove to the airport and lined up a couple of cabs, and then there they all were! Straggling through the chaos looking tired and dishevelled, all except Liberty.

My daughter Liberty is a supermodel. She is able to look cool and beautiful under all circumstances, and she was doing so now, despite the fact that they had lost her luggage.

Her husband Rupert, himself a film director and no mere lap animal, was left to sort out the missing bags and any other problems. He was waving his arms and speaking in Spanish, to no avail. The crowds parted and Liberty emerged. She rushed forward and hugged her mum.

'Mum. Mum. Dad.' The others gathered round. The ones who live in America hadn't seen Bunty for a while. Milo and Holly, who live in London, were herding their kids towards one of the taxis. Atticus, our eldest, was having some sort of intense discussion with his wife Claudia, carried on in hissing whispers. They are both Goths, and looked particularly thin and pale against the backdrop of bronzed southern Italians. Leo, our youngest, also thin and pale, long and lanky, stood beside his mum playing idly with her hair.

Mia appeared with her American husband Taylor and their baby daughter Finch.

Milo and Holly, meanwhile, had got into a fight about car seats. Holly had brought a car seat with her but Alitalia had lost it. Milo hadn't brought one, but I had, in the Clio, for his youngest, Ludo. This left Holly's youngest, Lincoln, car-seatless, even though she had gone to all the trouble of bringing one.

'Dad brought that for Ludo,' Milo was saying, his arms folded in an uncompromising manner.

'It's not fair,' said Holly. 'It's not my fault Alitalia lost it.'

'It's not my fault either. Lincoln will just have to sit on your lap.'

The taxi driver was watching all this in bewilderment, car seats being virtually unknown in Calabria, where infants are carried on the handlebars of Vespas.

Then Lincoln and Ludo themselves began fighting, and Holly's elder child Gypsy started crying.

'Dad,' Holly called across the melee and bedlam of Italian travellers.

I reluctantly made my way towards the scene of conflict, the first of many no doubt, not convinced of the importance of the car seat, but knowing Holly was, and that Milo was probably just digging in his heels for the hell of it.

'Come on, guys!' I said. 'Here we are in sunny Calabria! All those silly London things don't matter down here, that's the beauty of it.'

'Cars still crash, don't they?' said Holly, with the kind of irrefutable logic that defies diplomacy.

I decided to try a different tack with Milo, on the whole a softer target. 'Come on, old chap, it's not that far. Ludo can sit on your lap.'

'It's not my fault they lost her car seat.'

'Yes, but she did bring one, if you see what I mean.'

He saw what I meant, and that the disputed car seat was in my car and therefore under my control. And, as I added, sotto voce, man to man, who cares anyway? It was probably the only car seat in the whole of Reggio.

Milo's wife Honey, whose mum lives in Tuscany, more familiar than the rest with Italian ways, agreed, clinching things.

Meanwhile whatever luggage that hadn't been lost was piling up on the sidewalk and being loaded by the drivers. The passengers piled in after it and the cavalcade finally moved off.

I took Holly and the children in the car-seated Clio, and their reaction as we swung through the villa gates made all the aggravation worthwhile. From there the drive slopes straight to the sea, which shimmered under the hot sky like a picture postcard of the perfect holiday.

'The sea!' cried Gypsy.

'Cool!' said Lincoln.

'My God, Dad! This place is fantastic.'

The professore's works were not yet visible, hidden at this point by the oleander hedge and the tunnel of pines that shade the drive. Only when we emerged in front of the house was the full eyesore revealed.

It being in the nature of children to focus only on important things, the two of them noticed nothing but the low wall over which they clambered and jumped down onto the sandy beach shrieking with excitement.

Holly was diplomatic. I'd prepared her for the worst in the car. 'It's not *that* bad, Dad. Maybe you could grow some trees or something.' One of the workmen waved and another one whistled at her.

'The sooner the better,' I heartily agreed.

'They'd have to be awfully tall though.'

This gloomy fact was only too obvious, and we were both musing on it when the cabs arrived and began to disgorge their human cargo.

Reactions were mixed, as you might expect, between the splendour of our premises and the proximity of the professore's monstrosity. Diplomacy fought with candour, according to who was expressing it.

Atticus, my eldest, educ. Eton, has the unique OE worldview and satirical manner of expressing it. He surveyed the scene meticulously, taking it all in, as an officer might a battlefield, searching for tactical advantage: 'Couldn't you build a wall or something, Dad? You'd be between him and the sun – you could block his light.'

'I'm not sure I want a war – I'm the outsider down here. I don't want to end up being ethnically cleansed.'

'You'll have to do something.'

'Yes – trees or something.'

'Or a hedge – a really massive hedge. Leylandii maybe, really fast-growing.'

And so the first seeds of an idea were sown – an idea that was to blossom later that year into the Immense Fence.

Milo, in contrast, second in line, a San Fernando Valley high school dropout and surfer dude, had eyes only for the beach, and his reaction was similar to Lincoln's. The professore's house was a mere periphery. I wished I could cultivate such tunnel vision myself.

'Dad, this place is amazing! This is the coolest thing you've ever done.' And he leapt over the wall, removed his outer garments and swam off in search of anything that might resemble a wave.

When Liberty emerged there was considerable whistling from the rooftop. She approached them with her hands on her hips.

'Shut *up!*' she said.

They didn't understand English but they got the message. Sheepishly they obeyed and resumed their interminable hammering, preparing the vast slope of the prof's roof for its tegoli – the traditional Italian roof tile.

Mia drew the boathouse bedroom, which was thought best for the baby, and for the increased privacy the bedroom would bring. Her new husband Taylor is an American, from the Deep South, and therefore quite conservative. It was thought that exposure to the worst excesses of our family life at close quarters might prove a bit much for him at such an early stage in his marriage. Children have a way of behaving that can bring a blush to even a hardened cheek like mine. For example one afternoon I witnessed a scene between Ludo and Taylor, roughly as follows:

Ludo was standing naked on a garden table peeing into a flowerbed.

Taylor told him he thought this was 'inappropriate'.

Ludo said, 'I don't know what that means,' and went on peeing.

All the others squashed into the remaining space somehow, mainly by laying out kids toe-to-toe in bunks, and on the Ikea sofa surrounding the television, an arrangement that proved extremely popular.

Bunty and I withdrew into the barakka, and tried not to think about how everyone was going to manage. In the humid darkness sinister scrabbling sounds on the roof soon took our minds off it. Were they inside or out?

Next day Atticus, his wife Claudia, Taylor and Leo all announced they would have to leave early, unexpectedly needed back in California. I could hardly blame them,

Leo, identifiable on sight as a musician, long and thin as only rockers can be, and dressed entirely in black, for some reason attracted Gianni's attention from the outset. Gianni came round, greeted everybody effusively, kissed them all, especially the girls, then invited Leo on a fishing trip in his boat.

This was a first for Gianni, and an undoubted honour, and we all urged Leo to go. Leo has little or no interest in the sea, boats or fish (except sushi). But on the other hand he is a master, if not of the fishing line, of the line of least resistance. And this line now drew him inexorably to his doom.

Before they left Gianni decided on a test run round the bay, this being the boat's first outing that season, really a way of giving all the children a ride before the main event.

They clambered excitedly aboard around Leo, a pale and not entirely enthusiastic Pied Piper, and off they went across the placid blue bay. We concerned adults stood on the beach, from where we could hear their happy cries clearly across the water.

Suddenly the cries turned to shrieks of fear and horror, and we could see them all jumping around in the lurching boat. The boat made several drunken zigzagging arcs, then headed rapidly for shore, white foam creaming from its bows.

As soon as it crunched ashore the children leapt into the water, led by five-year-old Gypsy, screaming hysterically up the beach to her mother, her face contorted with terror.

'Whatever *is* it, Gypsy?' Holly grabbed the trembling girl, herself freaked-out in the face of such horror.

But Gypsy could only howl and groan.

Milo's boys, once safely out of danger, explained, 'A *rat.*'

'It was absolutely *huge*!'

'It jumped into the *sea.*'

'And swam *away.*'

'It was in the *engine.*'

Gianni meanwhile was holding his sides laughing. 'Grande topo,' he kept saying. 'Topo di mare. Topo in motore.'

A rat, apparently, had made its winter nest in the depths of the engine, and was understandably alarmed when the thing started rumbling into life around it. It shot, according to the account later compiled from the eyewitnesses once they'd simmered down, straight up in the air, landed in the boat, raced around for a while (hence the rocking and rolling), before leaping headlong into the sea. For a group of novice mariners it could hardly have been a more dramatic introduction.

Leo remained on board, looking slightly shell-shocked. You could see he wanted to disembark, but just as he rose to his feet to do so two barrel-chested Calabrese, Gianni's fishing mates, rolled up with all sorts of equipment and started loading it aboard, trapping him among the nets and lines.

As the boat set off once more, this time rapidly over the horizon, he turned and waved, more than a little wistfully. Not speaking a word of Italian, it was hard to imagine how he would get through what promised, and indeed turned out to be, an extremely long day.

Night was falling when at last the sound of a puttering engine was heard, echoing across the starry water, and Gianni's masthead light hove into view.

Leo came trailing up the beach, his body language that of a broken man, and joined us by the barbecue, where Rupert, a great one for camp-fire leadership, had taken command of the evening meal.

'What, no fish for the pot, Leo?' said Rupert.

Leo shook his head speechlessly. They hadn't caught any fish. Just sunstroke.

It was some time before he could talk of his ordeal, not a happy introduction to the Old Mediterranean Way of Life as far as he was concerned.

15

La Musica

Leo was soon under pressure once more, this time from another quarter, having caught the attention of Pino. It being August, he and his family were living in their beach house full time, and there was nothing they liked better than a musical evening, preferably gathered round a beach bonfire.

He had spotted Leo for the guitarist he was, and there seemed no way of explaining to him the difference between electric guitars in rock bands, and strumming out Calabrian folk tunes acoustically, accompanied by children on innocent instruments like tambourines and an accordion.

Leo, once bitten by Gianni, tended to disappear at the first sign of Pino, and it was left to me to make increasingly lame-sounding excuses. The language barrier didn't help, as usual the enemy of anything in the way of subtle arguments and complex bullshit.

'Elettrica, elettrica' I kept saying, accompanied by heavy-metal gestures. But he didn't seem to know anything about rock bands. Viviana liked 'Sk8er Boi' by Avril Lavigne, but that was about as far as it went. The decadent world of Anglo-American rock seemed to be a closed book.

Nevertheless there was to be a singsong on the beach below our house, which there was no way of avoiding. Pino announced that he would dig the hole and gather the driftwood for the fire. We would provide a suitable barbecue feast. The date was set.

Rupert said that what we really needed for this and other occasions was a long table suitable for family feasts and similar large gatherings. We could make one ourselves out of wood.

When Pasquale heard about this he shook his head knowingly. Inglesis would not be capable of such a task. But Rupert is a relentless DIY artist, and had brought his tool kit. The battlelines were drawn.

We needed Pasquale's help to get the wood, which meant him necessarily becoming a kind of consultant. Nothing Calabrian is ever simple, and in this case I suspected him of making things even more complicated than usual.

How wide would the tabletop be? How thick, how long? What about the legs? What height did we want the table? If it was for a family, perhaps the size of the children ought to be considered. None of us really knew the standard height for a table when we came to think about it. In fact we didn't know the answers to any of Pasquale's infuriating questions, which was just the way he wanted it.

Smoking his usual steady stream of cigarettes, Pasquale came as close as he could to taking over the project. But Rupert wasn't having it. He stood his ground. Nicknamed 'The Colonel', accustomed to ordering film crews and actors and all manner of temperamental types to do his bidding, he wasn't going to be beaten by a Calabrese upstart like Pasquale.

Pasquale, equally, didn't like to see valuable work slipping away into the hands of amateurs. There remained his trump card, the wood, and the fact that it came from Nino di Palizzi's yard, where the cutting would necessarily be done, and where he would have the upper hand.

We all gathered there one hot afternoon with Nino and various onlookers, not one of whom didn't have an opinion as to the dimensions of tables.

One thing swiftly became clear: the length of table we wanted would sag in the middle. A middle row of legs was ruled out, and it was Mia who came up with the simple solution: we would make two tables.

There wasn't much anyone could say against this, especially since it came from an attractive young female. The Calabrese scratched themselves and said, 'Bravo, bravo.'

The wood for the tops was simple enough, and was soon selected. Length and width was an issue, of course, but nothing like the issue of the legs. The legs took us into truly disputative territory. Who would have thought something as simple as a table leg could be so complicated? Even when the height had finally been agreed (or rather disagreed – there were notable dissenters), there remained the critical question of how to make the ends straight and level. If they weren't absolutely so, the table would wobble.

Rupert, a perfectionist, insisted on examining Nino's equipment. He did so with a critical eye, which didn't go down well at all. The idea that he couldn't cut straight edges with his buzz saw was an affront to Nino's dignity.

I wished Rupert would temper his remarks with a little diplomacy, but he is more ruthless than me, and making the perfect table had become a major challenge, especially since Pasquale had thrown down the gauntlet.

The whole thing looked like breaking into outright war, with some of the onlookers muttering darkly, when Pasquale himself healed the breach by saying he would take the legs to the carpentiere, who had the necessary special tool, and anyway was a master carpenter.

Nobody wanted to argue with this, and Pasquale loaded the legs into his car like so many trophies of war. He drove off with his booty, a triumphant smile on his face, puffing his ciggy.

Everyone joined in for the final assembly, having first signed the bottoms of the tabletops for posterity. Then Honey, who is an artist, painted the tops with shells and starfish and other aquatic delights, and the little kids added their handprints for good measure.

Mia with her set-designing skills was a frontrunner with Rupert, hammering in the smooth-ended legs, bracing them with struts, all under the watchful eye of Pasquale, who by now regarded them with fierce personal interest, almost like children, even though they were, he said, too short: 'troppo breve'.

There was something intensely sceptical about the way he puffed his ciggy when Table One was upended onto its legs for the first time. We all stood around in breathless anticipation: would it wobble?

'Hooray!' A ragged cheer went up – the thing was solid as a rock. Pasquale was quick to take the credit for the non-wobbly legs and joined in the general hugging.

The other one was just as good and they fitted together like jigsaw, between them a table fit for any banquet and ready in time for the forthcoming feast with the Pinos.

We gave the thing a test run that lunchtime and if anything it was too high. After all Pasquale's dark predictions, the children's chins were all balanced on the edge like so many Oliver Twists, especially when the gelati came around.

But the thing about children is that they grow, and meanwhile cushions can be stuffed under them. That was the general consensus. The idea of taking the legs off again and shortening them was a definite bridge too far.

For the Great Day we ordered steaks and breaded chicken and sausages and lamb kebabs from the marcelleria in the village, with Gianni adding a triumphant last-minute large tonno he'd caught that afternoon.

Pino appeared and started digging the hole, and Rupert took charge of the barbecue, surrounded by his sous-chefs, me included. A huge August moon was rising in the aquamarine twilight, laying a path of gold across the water as the charcoal began to whiten. The aromatic wood smoke rose, and Rupert ordered that the first meats – the kebabs and sausages – be prepared for immediate griddling. An idyllic scene, you might think.

Until an ear-splitting scream rent the air. Bunty, no longer sitting but standing and jumping about on the wall, was pointing in horror at the boathouse olive tree. I followed her trembling fingers.

A rat was running down it – a large, long-tailed country rat – followed by another rat and then another, all about the size of miniature kangaroos. Judging by the expertness of their descent it was clear this was a well-worn path to wherever they were going, in this case along the bottom of the wall on which Bunty was hopping.

'They obviously like the smell of sizzling sausages,' said Rupert. 'They want to join in the barbie.'

There was no doubt that this was where they were heading. They ducked behind the barbecue and seemed to disappear.

The barbecue, a simple structure of stone slabs, backs onto the sea wall, where there are plenty of holes and drains and things, as well as a prolific vine, ideal cover for a rat, even one as big as these.

For those working in close proximity – except Rupert, who took them in his stride, treating them almost as unexpected guests – it was unnerving to say the least, thinking of them behind there, out of sight, ready to jump out at any moment with their nasty, gnashing teeth. I don't really like rats, or snakes, or even lizards for that matter, especially when they get into the house and appear on the ceiling above your bed in the middle of the night.

Our snakes are meant to be harmless, but you wouldn't want to cuddle one. Gerald Durrell would probably like them, but not me. The Italian word is serpente, marvellously Biblical and slithery-sounding – the very word seems to hiss. They say they eat the rats, but this evening it was clear they weren't eating nearly enough of them.

Pino joined us, attracted by the screams.

'Tranquillo, Bunty!' he said, putting a protective arm around her. 'Sono solo topi di campagna.' These were country rats, living, like us, in a rustic place. What could be more natural?

At this moment a voice, peevish and testy, rang out across the professor's hedge:

'PING PONG, PING PONG!'

There was no mistaking the jarring note.

Pino said, 'Ignore.'

The ping pong match the boys were playing continued for a short while, until a victory and the arrival of the first wave of food terminated it. There was no need either to obey or disobey our diabolical neighbour.

'*He* can complain about our ping pong, but there's nothing *we* can do about his beastly house,' said Bunty bitterly.

'I'll think of something,' I said, with more bravado than conviction.

Celeste and the children arrived and admired the new table. We all sat down, and for a while at least the rats and the professore were forgotten.

Except by me. I was still sensitive, my immunity to fresh shocks damaged, like bruised fruit, and two new blows did nothing to improve my appetite. Rats in the shadows making scratching noises were one thing, and disturbing enough. But out in the open, bold as brass, joining in the festivities like pet dogs – next thing they'd be jumping on our laps. I looked down nervously. In the darkness beneath the table it was hard to tell what might be lurking there.

It was also hard to focus on the Calabrese fare the family had prepared, adding to the barbecue traditional dishes like ciambotta, a favourite local way of cooking melanzane (aubergine), with red peppers, potatoes and tomatoes; antipasti locale using Gianni's tuna in various creative ways learned from our local Mama Papa restaurant; and a local pasta dish, spaghetti al ragu di totano. The meal was rounded off with a sweet pasta dessert, dolce con pasta frolla.

My mind was so distracted with rats and with the latest annoyance from the professore, that it was hard to get the most out of this tremendous culinary effort to impress our guests.

But the mood overall was mellow by the time we hit the beach and gathered round the fire for the traditional singsong.

'Leo, Leo,' Pino called, as he strummed the first chords of the tarantella rhythm on his chitarra battente and Dario squeezed out the opening bars on his accordion. But of the great guitarist there was no sign. In the deep shadows around the flickering fire it was impossible to say who was there and who wasn't, but if he was he was keeping quiet about it.

The moon-path was silver, the lapping shoals celestial as the fire embers dwindled at last, and La Musica languished into a final lullaby.

For those who wanted more (and for those who didn't) there was an announcement from Pino. In two evenings' time there was to be a music festival in Bova Superiore. We were all welcome – in reality obliged – to come. For those who didn't want more it was too bad. We would be heading up into the mountains on Friday night whether we liked it or not.

Calabrese folk music is, like the New Folk Movement globally, very much alive and kicking. The older traditionalists have been joined by a new generation of La Musica lovers, which in Calabria does seem to mean the majority, rather than the minority who like folk in most other countries. Down here in the Mezzogiorno they haven't been corrupted by Western ways, or seduced from their impromptu caffé concertos by MTV. They make their own music and it keeps them pure, like creatures on the Galapagos Islands.

We set off in a convoy led by Pino, some crammed into his space-wagon, others into Gianni's estate car, others into the Clio. Mothers with young children stayed behind. Milo and Leo rode with me in the one car that could be used for an early-exit strategy, should that become desirable. We'd heard an awful lot of Calabrese music already that week.

Bova Superiore, spread over a hilltop like icing on a fairy cake, is one of those places you see a long time before you get to it. It keeps appearing and disappearing as you wind around the mountain. Sometimes you're almost there, only to find next time round you're actually further away.

This went on for quite a while as dusk fell, a violet afterglow shimmering between the glowing tips of the mountains and the deep shadow of the valleys below.

Lights were beginning to twinkle in medieval windows, reflecting on the shiny cobbles of narrow twisting streets, as we made our way finally into the heart of the town, the piazza, floodlit backdrop for the evening's festivities.

Before we got there we passed a large steam locomotive, parked in a side street on a short section of track. When we'd parked we asked Pino what it was doing there.

'Some time ago one mayor of Bova, perhaps a little crazy, thought this engine might bring many tourists to the town.'

'Perhaps a little "loco"?' Milo quipped.

'But it doesn't go anywhere,' I said.

'No, no,' said Pino, as if this went without saying, 'much too steep up the mountains.'

A church, the town hall and a café fronted onto three sides of the piazza, against the fourth side of which a large stage had been built, backing onto gardens, in the shadows of which some of the younger folk were already larking and creeping about, whistling in the dark for girlfriends who, judging by the look of the mothers, were unlikely ever to join them.

On the stage a folk group, the first of many, was warming up. Prominent among them was an elderly lady seated on a stool, all but overwhelmed by her zampogna, a Calabrese bagpipe with double-chanted drones, the wind for which is supplied by an enormous goat hide, removed from the slaughtered animal in one piece and tied off at the legs, with one rear leg used to house the blowpipe.

Into this she now blew, swelling the bag to a size that almost swamped her and causing Leo to remark:

'Two old bags.'

Out of the corner of my eye I saw Celeste, standing the other side of Leo from me, and I knew from her expression that she'd heard, and understood the literal translation if not the humour. He was already on thin ice with the Pinos for repeatedly ducking his guitar duties.

The group struck up a tarantella, which went on for quite a while. Then the old lady made an extremely lengthy speech, presumably announcing the next number. But when it came it sounded, to us at least, exactly the same as the first one. Then, unbelievable as it may seem, they played it a third time. This was when we sloped off to find something to eat.

Pino was upset because the tables he'd booked hadn't been kept for us at the little restaurant he'd been going on about for days. When we arrived, there was a lot of shrugging, culminating in Pino waving his arms and shouting at the maître d'.

It was a shame because the place looked much nicer than his usual barn-like eateries, cosy and bustling, with tables outside, around which delicious cooking smells wafted on the warm night air.

His plan B was for us to assemble around his spacewagon in a small parking lot where, after a considerable interval, he appeared at the head of his family, all of them carrying plates piled with sausages.

They were very welcome, but we all knew they didn't make up for the disappointment. I wondered what could have happened. Some political rival, perhaps, had booked the place out to score off him? I remembered the night of the pig festival. Pino did have his enemies, some of them more than ready to play rough.

When the main body began to drift back to the piazza, Milo, Leo and I, and now Atticus, found ourselves involuntarily lagging behind. The Clio was strategically parked in a side street, with direct access to the wider world. Somehow or other, without really saying anything, we found ourselves in the car and I began reversing.

Before long the narrow streets, with their reverberations of tarantella music (same tune, different band) faded and were lost to sight and sound, and all that remained were the sweet evening smells of harvested mountain grass, rich with sun-dried oregano, and the deafening chatter of cicadas.

We drank this in through the car's open windows, not saying much. There wasn't much to say really. We'd heard more than enough tarantella music, but none of us wanted to actually say so. It might have seemed ungrateful, and vaguely disloyal, so we just enjoyed the silence. At that moment it was sweeter than any music.

16

Celebrity Kidnapping

It wasn't long before the *Mail on Sunday* was on the line, having tracked down Liberty. It was me who took the call from Sebastian O'Kelly, editor of the travel pages, which are really property pages plus celebs. The idea of Liberty Ross lounging on our unheard-of beach in her bikini was clearly getting him excited.

'Where are you exactly down there?' he said.

'Not far from Reggio, on the Ionian side.'

'South of Locri?'

'About sixty kms.'

'You must be mad.'

'How d'you mean?'

'My dear chap, you're in *bandit country*.'

'It doesn't really affect us though – not so far anyway.'

'They've killed twenty-six politicians in Locri this year already.'

'They have?'

'And Liberty's just lying there?'

'She's on the beach right now, yes.'

'I'd love to get a photographer down there to take a look. Give your place a nice write-up.'

Where I made my mistake was this: Sebastian O'Kelly's honeyed words came as sweet music to my ears. My dreadful insecurities about having gone a bridge too far and ending up beyond the pale of the property market, still haunted me. The idea of a write-up, putting me on the map and vindicating my leap into the unknown, appealed to me like harts panting for cooling streams.

I strolled down to the beach where the womenfolk were lying.

'Rather good news,' I said.

Bunty said, 'Oh yes?' You could tell she was already suspicious.

'Yes. The *Mail on Sunday* want to do a piece on the place. Centre-page spread in the travel section – put us on the map. Should have a massive impact on the value, I should think. Want to send a photographer down right away.'

'They didn't mention Liberty, did they?'

'Well…'

'You idiot! You just don't get it, do you?'

'Don't get what?'

'All they're after is free pictures of Liberty without going through Storm.'

'Oh I think that's nonsense. He sounded really interested in the idea of us being down here in what he called *bandit country.*'

'Bandit country?'

'That's what he called it when I told him where we were.'

'Oh that's just great, isn't it? Alert the mafia! Rich pickings in Spropoli.'

'It's not a question of alerting the mafia – it's just a good story, that's all. Anyway they've given up kidnapping.'

'How do you know?'

'I just do.'

'So you don't just want to wreck her career by handing out free pictures to the tabloids, you don't care if she gets kidnapped as well?'

'They've given *up* kidnapping.'

'They can always take it up again, can't they? Especially when they see a sitting duck in the paper, right on their own doorstep.'

'I don't expect they read the *Mail on Sunday.*'

Liberty rolled over on her tummy and said, 'Dad, it's okay. All you have to do is tell the guy to come down and take pictures of the house, but not me. Tell him I've gone to Paris or something.'

'He won't believe it.'

'That's not the point. You need to find out if he's still interested in this brilliant thing you've done without anything to do with me.'

'Yes,' said her mother. 'That's fair enough, isn't it? Put him on the spot – see what he's *really* after.'

I rang Sebastian O'Kelly: 'As it turns out Liberty won't be here after all. She's had to go to Paris.'

'That was a bit sudden, wasn't it?'

'You know how it is with these models – always jetting off somewhere.'

'So there's absolutely no chance of any pictures of her?'

'Absolutely none.'

'Tell you what then – how about an interview over the phone?'

'Who with?'

'With Liberty of course!'

'But Liberty doesn't know anything about down here – why we came and so forth. You said yourself it's really interesting, the idea of someone going beyond the pale of tourism. I don't think Liberty's terribly up on the finer points of southern Italy.'

'All the same – it would be interesting to get her take on it.'

'Look, Sebastian, it's just not going to happen. Surely you can talk about travel and property without there always having to be some celebrity angle?'

'I could, but my readers would far rather I didn't. They like to think they're following in the footsteps of trendsetters like your daughter.'

'Why not just interview me? You might as well – I'm the only one who's going to do it anyway.'

'I already have interviewed you.'

'And the pix?'

'The paper won't pay for a long trip like that without a pot of gold at the end of it. There isn't even a direct flight. There'll be hotel bills and Christ knows what.'

'By pot of gold you mean Liberty?'

'Leave it with me – I've got the general idea. I can dig up some pix of the Jasmine Coast – it'll be a nice piece, I promise you.'

I returned to the beach to make my report.

'All sorted!' I said.

'And?'

'And it's absolutely fine about Liberty. He quite understands. He's interviewed me at length about coming here and southern Italy and everything, so much so he doesn't even need to send a photographer.'

'I told you he wouldn't without Liberty.'

'He doesn't *need* to – that's all. He says it will be a really nice piece using pictures of the Jasmine Coast. So there you are! We're going to be on the map.'

Liberty said, 'I think we're better off *off* the map. Somewhere nobody knows about, you said – no dreadful tourists demanding fish and chips, you said.'

'Yes I did say that. But sometimes I long for one of those cafés like they have in Rome – marbletop tables, waiters in long white aprons.'

'Chip shop's what you'll get the way you're going,' said Bunty.

When they got back to London a few weeks later they were just in time for the 'piece'. That very Sunday they opened the *Mail* to be greeted by an enormous picture of Liberty, full-page size, superimposed on a short story about how her daddy had bought a place in Bandit Country with cash stuffed down his trousers.

After the deserters returned to sunny California we settled down to a routine, the way you do on holiday: breakfast, lunch, shopping, kids yelling, everyone arguing, evening swimming, supper, games, bed.

Once we were just the remainers it was easier to spread out and do our own thing. Liberty's first own thing was to tackle the timetable of the professore's workers, who began their hammering at the ungodly hour of seven a.m.

She marched up to the fence in her bikini, more than enough to get their attention. A hush fell, into which she spoke, pointing at her wrist.

'Too EARLY. Too much NOISE. Start LATER, maybe eight – OTTO.'

The silence on the roof became a murmuring as the astonished men consulted each other. They gradually got back to normal, but next morning at seven there was no sign of them. A blissful silence reigned until well after eight, by which time children and coffee addicts like me were up anyway, and breakfast was under way.

Liberty walked over and thanked them, and after that they were putty in her hands.

The following Saturday we all went into Palizzi for ice cream at our favourite gelateria, Roberta's, facing the piazza. As well as gelati and delicious pastries Roberta's is a bar and the focal point of town life. Here the old 'pensiones' gather from breakfast onwards to sip grappa and coffee and exchange views or just do nothing, occasionally popping into Roberta's annexe next door which is filled with gaming machines.

A popular myth grew easily in our family that these old geezers were retired mafia hitmen. They certainly looked the part, with their bling and their rings and their chins on their sticks.

That day when we arrived in the piazza further evidence of this threat to our safety was provided by some alarming graffiti. Scrawled in red on the wall of the building opposite were the words 'Inglesi Assassini'.

'Just something to do with football I should think,' I said, playing it down as best I could.

All the same I noticed Holly put on her shades and pull down her sun hat.

While we were sitting there in the sunshine, enjoying our ice creams and being stared at by the old hitmen, a wedding got underway outside the piazza church. A huge white Rolls Royce and about fifteen matching black BMWs all swept past in convoy.

As far as Bunty was concerned there was no doubt. This was a mafia wedding, 'just like in *The Godfather*'.

'You don't know that,' I said.

'Of course it is.'

Next day Pasquale, who lives in Palizzi and is a regular habitué of Roberta's, came by. 'Did you see that wedding yesterday?' I asked.

He looked a bit blank.

'Grande matrimonio ieri, chiesa di piazza. Was it the mafia?' I muttered the word sotto voce, with a small m.

Pasquale smiled, spread his hands and shook his head. Looking me straight in the eye, he said, 'Mafia? Non ho capito mafia.'

No one I know down there seems to have heard of them.

August drew to a close, heralding the end of the holiday and the return to work and school. Sudden summer storms, over in minutes, foreshadowed September weather. Everything was changing.

The family had been there for five weeks and the settled rhythm in the soporific heat was hard to break. Routine had completely taken over and even the rows had almost ended.

Before they left we decided to have a grande festa for everyone we knew. All were invited, even the professore. To get the party going, Rupert made gallons of strawberry and vodka hooch that blew your head off. None of the Calabrese drank a drop of it, preferring only wine and beer in very modest quantities. I think it was something to do with the family nature of the occasion, that decorum demanded sobriety in front of wives and children and the hard drinking ways of the hunting party were saved for Men Only days.

We cooked a Calabrian fish soup called zuppa del pescatori, made antipasto misto using strong local salamis with baby tomatoes and sardo (a sheep's milk cheese made originally in Sardinia); wild boar cutlets specially ordered from our marcelleria for the occasion, cooked on the barbecue with seared aubergine slices, served with boiled baby zucchini; and macaroni with local funghi and green peas.

Holly and Honey excelled themselves with their home-made olive bread, baked with dried oregano which we found growing wild on the hillside behind the flats where the barking dogs lived.

Everybody and more turned up: Nino with two enormous sons, the professore and his wife with two little grand-daughters who'd been playing with Ludo on the beach every day, and a friend who owned an olive grove and contributed a huge flagon of oil.

It was a bit like the Feeding of the Five Thousand, but in the end a resounding triumph, with the Pino family providing La Musica long into the night. Everybody danced under the stars until the children were asleep in their seats. Then the Italians went home.

No one would have thought there was the slightest friction between us as the professore gallantly kissed Mia goodbye. Everyone hugged and kissed and wished each other well until l'anno prossimo.

In the morning Pino and Gianni helped me drive everyone to the airport. As we gathered on the concourse I felt like it was me going back to school – that weird airy feeling that catches in your throat.

Left behind again I hugged Bunty until she could hardly breathe.

'If only we could do something normal for a change,' I said.

'Do something about the professore's house,' she replied, as soon as she could get her breath. 'That's what you've got to do.'

17

The Green Vote

September, my second in Calabria, turned warm and mellow after the August heat, a languid, lazy, burnt-out month of early grape harvests and cool evenings, washed by occasional torrential downpours that streaked the hillsides with green, and drew aromatic pungency from the pines and herbs that covered them, filling the air with the scent of myrtle and wild thyme.

This became even more pronounced when I went up into the mountains.

High in the hills above Bova Superiore, higher than anything I'd imagined, are fertile plateaux, hidden away like Lost Worlds. Irrigated by lakes fed by the springs and melting snows of the Aspromonte, they are the habitat of large commercial fruit farms.

I'd never imagined such places could exist in so arid a climate, and never would have known about them had I not gone there with Pino in his quest for the Green Vote.

It all started when Tarka arrived with his girlfriend Carolina.

I was just settling down to a short period of much-needed solitude, gazing out to sea and wondering how on earth I'd ever get Pasquale and co. back to work on the wooden house after their long layoff, when down the drive came an unexpected small, shiny car.

Nothing new about that, of course. My life is punctuated by unexpected arrivals. Much more unexpected were the occupants.

Tarka is the son of my old chum Denny, legendary producer of rock'n'roll classics like 'Whiter Shade of Pale', and the person who introduced me to the joys of living on the beach in Malibu.

Tarka takes after him in that he leads a 1960s lifestyle, never grew up, follows that dream, etc. He plays guitar, writes songs, believes the Rolling Stones are semi-divine and has excellent taste in girlfriends. One of them was with him now, in the process of uncoiling herself from the passenger seat.

'Hey, Flipper – meet Carolina!' (He calls me Flipper, my sometime nickname. His father and I ran Flipper's, the rollerskating nightclub in Hollywood.)

Carolina was an eyeful and then some: friendly, willowy, honey-coloured, cascading hair – rather like a mermaid with legs. She smiled and said 'Hello' with an American accent.

Carolina was from New York. Rather than walk she seemed to undulate.

'Just thought we'd come and see how you're doing,' said Tarka.

'I'm glad you did,' I said. It *was* a bit weird without the family, come to think of it.

'This place is great! What's that funky old thing over there?'

'That's the barakka.'

'That's *so* Escondido Beach.'

'Yes, and it's got an old tree and a beach shower, just like your dad's. First thing I saw here. Made me think of Malibu right away.'

'Mind if we take a look?'

'Feel free.'

Tarka and Carolina liked it so much they moved in right away. With its rudimentary kitchen, you can live in the barakka without further reference to the outside world, which was what they wanted – beach and bed – a honeymoon without a wedding, feeding on the fruits of life.

Whenever they felt satiated they would emerge and we'd sally forth to Padreterno, our local Mama Papa restaurant in the village.

Padreterno is everything a rustic Italian restaurant should be. If it were magically transported to London or New York there'd be lines round the block. As it is, in Galati, the burial place of the Greek Queen (I'm not sure where she's buried – no one seems to know), you know it's open if the Mama's ancient mother is sitting outside on her chair, a bit like a goat tethered to a stake to attract a tiger. When they close they pull her in again. If she's not there and you're really hungry, if you bang loudly enough they'll usually come and rustle something up.

But it's best when they're open, because that means the pizza oven, a massive thing that dominates the room, second only to the television, is fired up with fragrant olive wood, ready to bake the crunchiest, most delicious pizza you've ever had in your life.

Tarka, like his father, always fussy about his food, immediately realised we were onto something special. He scanned the long list of pizzas with a discerning eye, under the approving gaze of the Mama, who'd obviously taken a shine to him. Then he said he wanted something different.

That's when I discovered Carolina spoke Italian. She was an Italian-American girl, raised on pasta as well as promises, with a full-blood Tuscan mother.

She explained that Tarka wanted his pizza with spinach and a fried egg.

The Mama, built on the lines of a seaside fat lady, who you might have expected to be put out by this, seemed overjoyed by Tarka's inventiveness.

'Bravo, bravo,' she said, 'bravissima idea!' her mighty forearms folded archly over her starched white apron.

We sat outside on the terrace overlooking the garden, where they grow vegetables, lemons and olives, all presumably for the pot.

While we waited for our pizzas she produced a steady stream of antipasti: aubergine and zucchini fried in delicious batter, home-made salamis with capers, white bean and tuna salad, bruschetta di casa (toasted ciabatta bread with mashed tomatoes, garlic and basil), prosciutto crudo with figs, mini-frittatas, olive tapenade, fresh mozzarella with capers and garlic, grilled mozzarella, goat cheese with sun dried tomatoes, cucumbers filled with tuna, ricotta crostini, broiled fresh figs and dates, calamari fritti, marinated mushrooms stuffed into aubergine, and freshly baked focaccia bread served with dishes of delicious little olives which Tarka immediately got excited about.

'The skins on these olives are deliciously tough and tasty, have you noticed?'

I hadn't, to be honest. An olive is an olive, green or black. Unless it's stuffed, of course.

Tarka said, 'We should find out the name of these olives – maybe you can get some.'

'Can't I just buy some from her?'

'No, I mean a *tree.*'

The idea of planting an olive tree immediately seemed a magical thing to do. We munched it over and determined to speak to Gianni about where young trees could be found. With Carolina on board communications promised to be greatly improved.

This turned out to be an understatement. Gianni's reaction to Carolina was itself little short of mystical, like a novice meeting Aphrodite for the first time. When she spoke to him in Italian I thought he was going to swoon away. She was wearing her yellow bikini at the time, her trademark garment, a very minimal affair which emphasised her generous curves in such a way that Gianni – or any other red-blooded male for that matter – found it difficult to cope at close quarters.

Her warm skin seemed to radiate a glow of such headiness that Gianni, faced with so much of it, was plainly having problems articulating, but in the end he managed it.

'He says there are seven different kinds of olive trees you should buy,' Carolina translated.

A strip of land beyond the orchard parallel with the professore's fence seemed the ideal place for seven olive trees, which one day might grow big enough to screen at least a portion of the horrors beyond.

Seven is a lucky number, and when we measured it out we found it was ideal for the exact distance between each tree, a measurement of mystical as well as practical importance, since the olive tree is still seen, as Sophocles put it, as 'the tree that feeds the children', a sacred icon of Mediterranean culture since pre-historic times, especially here in Greek Bovesia, where pagan myth haunts the ancient hills that people still depend on for succour.

Gianni said, 'Destino.' And we all agreed.

September is a good month for planting, he said, before the rains come to irrigate the new roots. He would take us in his estate car to the fruit tree guy.

Hidden away in the hills behind Brancaleone, down a lane and round a bend and very unexpectedly, acres of young trees suddenly appeared.

There was a locked gate and a hut with goats in it. When we rang the bell and rattled the gate some chickens appeared, clucking and pecking excitedly.

Of human habitation there was no sign until Gianni hooted his horn. Then a voice called faintly from within the miniature forest, soon followed by a small old man in blue overalls.

'Sera,' he said as he opened the gate.

'Buonasera,' we all replied.

I felt we were being let in on a secret by Gianni, no doubt bewitched by Carolina. This was no roadside retail outlet, of which there are plenty, like Franco, charging like the Light Brigade.

Here the baby trees were three or four euros, obviously the price paid locally by the Calabrese.

Carolina and Gianni explained to the little old man what we were after, including the kind that had inspired the enterprise. He made a series of journeys into the interior, and very soon all seven were assembled. His little old wife then appeared from nowhere, carrying a bottle of limoncello, with which it was essential we should toast our seven olive trees to bring them luck and plentiful harvests.

We drank it from little paper cups. Then, feeling light-headed and dazed, we loaded up, paid up, bade farewell and roared off, Gianni laughing recklessly and leering at Carolina in his mirror as he negotiated a series of high-speed bends.

In Brancaleone he insisted we stop at his favourite gelateria, run by his friend Antoinetta. I thought a coffee might be a good idea for him.

Gleaming glass cases of pasticcini – the best for miles around: puff pastry parcels of creamy goo in all shapes and sizes, colours from chocolate to shocking pink, pink and green meringues, layered sponge slices, and flaky millefoglie smothered in strawberries and bulging with cream. A fragrant haze of espresso hung over the glass and marble showcases, ornate and profoundly Italian.

Antoinetta welcomed us, deeply impressed by Carolina with her Tuscan Italian. Gianni led Carolina to the ice-cream counter, while Tarka and I gazed at the pasticcini. Gianni, with his usual stubbornness, had got it into his head that we should all have his favourite treat, brioche stuffed with ice cream.

Eating this over-the-top concoction is a bit like being hit over the head with a blunt instrument, and on top of limoncello it promised to be hard to get over, even with multiple shots of espresso. Hardly a fit state for getting home and planting olive trees.

But Gianni insisted, so we waded through them – he was after all our host, something else he insisted on. I had pannacotta and tiramisu flavour in mine, Carolina pistachio and peach, which dribbled delightfully down her chin, so that Gianni was able to help her with a paper napkin.

When we got home he wouldn't hear of us helping with the planting. He dug seven holes, paced out to perfection, filled them with compost, sprinkled them with blue fertiliser pellets, then sank his hands up to the elbow, scooping the rich black mulch into hollows, soaking it with the hose, then settling the young olive trees into their beds. It was a splendid sight. Even though their trunks were little more than willow wands, their leaves twinkled in the evening sun with a hopeful gleam of rich harvests to come.

We thanked him admiringly. 'Prego,' he kept saying, 'niente.'

Then he kissed us all, especially Carolina.

Pino was still at the beach, and that weekend invited us all to lunch. Tarka took his guitar. Unlike Leo he was only too keen to regale them with his repertoire, which included almost the entire works of the Rolling Stones.

He made a big hit, as happy to join the family ensemble (Viviana on keyboards, Dario on accordion, Davide on guitar and Pino on his chitarra battente) and sing along with Calabrese folk as he was playing 'Angie', delivering the tortured lyrics with great theatricality, every inch the rock star he imagined himself to be.

The Pinos had no difficulty believing what he himself obviously believed, that he was 'resting his voice' after an American tour before starting a European one.

Carolina and I basked in the thing, both knowing it was total fantasy but no less enjoyable for it. That he could reel it off in front of us so glibly was more a testament to his deluded self-belief than to dishonesty. He had crossed the line that so many would like to cross, where life is a made-up story, and what's real is what you want it to be. In the Pinos' sunny courtyard, heady with home-made pizza and vino locale, almost anything seemed credible.

And for me it was all bravo. At last I'd produced a guitarist who would cooperate. He charmed them all afternoon, allowing me for once to relax and be a bystander. Carolina, from magical New York City, prevented those long silences that tend to occur when no one can think what to say or how to say it. Her fluent Italian, her Tuscan mother, her tales of the Big Apple, rendered her almost as exotic as Tarka himself. Pino is a big fish, but Bova is a very small pond by global standards.

Which brings us to the Green Vote and Pino's campaign to be mayor of Bova. At some point during the afternoon it must have occurred to him that Tarka and Carolina could be wheeled out on the hustings and presented as political props, a living testament to his international savoir-faire.

The following week he came by and asked if we'd join him on the campaign trail. When we agreed he asked Tarka to be sure and bring his guitar. The stage was set.

We started with a pass through Bova Marina, like a royal progress, with Pino a medieval monarch. As the car moved slowly through the town people surged forward and saluted him. Pino, his elbow out of the window, kept stopping to reach out his hand, not exactly to be kissed but almost, and say a few words.

'Ciao bella!'

Tarka muttered, 'I don't see how he can lose.' The thing seemed like a foregone conclusion, liable to end in a coronation rather than merely the town hall. Pino exuded charisma like an oriental potentate, his face suffused with an inner glow that elevated him from the merely mortal. The narrow streets echoed with his name, 'Pino, Pino, Pino!'

Then we headed into the hills.

Here the voters were more spread out, and the higher the winding road went into the mountains, the further down rough, precarious tracks they seemed to live. Pino was determined to leave no stone unturned in his pitch for the Green Vote, which he thought these rustic farmers embodied, a source hitherto untapped by his rivals, probably because it was such a problemo to get at.

The pitch was roughly the same at each venue. We would draw up and disembark. The voter would emerge, with wife, family, dogs, goats, etc. Hospitality would be offered and we'd all sit down, indoors or out. Pino would talk in a wise and reassuring way, while the wife poured whatever lethal concoction was on offer: home-made grappa, vino or limoncello. Small cakes usually came to soak it up, and coffee afterwards. The whole process was extremely lengthy, but this didn't bother Pino. 'Every Vote Counts' seemed to be his motto.

Carolina proved a big attraction, especially to the husbands, who would have voted for anything she said.

Tarka would strum a few bars to round things off when the politics were concluded. It went down well, his acoustic guitar and hippy appearance lending a distinctly green air, and a faint whiff of the Peace Movement, which chimed with Pino's role as the local chairman (they don't have chairpersons in Calabria) of Amnesty International.

And so eventually we wound our way up to the high plateaux above Bova Superiore, where the arid landscape suddenly turns green and you half expect one of Conan Doyle's *Lost World* dinosaurs to come lumbering out of the undergrowth.

The fertile vista stretched away like the alpine-style high pasture-lands of the Silas further north, where the ancient Greeks first came to graze their flocks and brought their culture to this wild Ionian shore.

The fruit trees grew in thousands around a central lake. A large farm complex and house could be seen nearby, home of the Very Important Person we had come to see.

'He has many workers,' said Pino, all of whom, it seemed, would swing behind their padrone and whatever candidate he favoured. We braced ourselves for a major effort.

We drove through the buildings, where stacks of boxes were being loaded onto lorries, and drew up by the house. An impressive terrace overlooked the vast panorama of apple trees below.

Steps led down from a side door in the house, at the bottom of which a table was laid next to an iron basket full of charcoal and olive wood smoking fragrantly under a metal griddle.

The grande padrone appeared – it could only be he – at the top of the steps, a tall grizzled figure with grey wavy hair and a Sicilian bandit moustache. He and Pino embraced warmly. Then we were introduced and invited to sit down. Wine bottles appeared. Then a lady in a long white apron came down the steps with a basket of fresh sardines and chucked them on the griddle. She drizzled them with olive oil and handfuls of chopped basil, and disappeared back up the steps. The smell of the sizzling sardines was delicious.

When the sardines were ready there was panelle to eat them with, a thing you rarely see outside Sicily. The lady in the apron, who turned out to be the padrone's wife, came back with a large platter of it which was handed round while her husband explained it was a dish that dated back to Arab times in Sicily, made of chickpea dough and fried in a vat of hot olive oil. 'Bellissima con sarde!'

Then came an antipasto of morzeddu Calabrese-style, made with home-made focaccia bread and home-cured pork. Tarka examined his meticulously, fascinated by every detail of each dish, which, through Carolina, he elicited from the padrone and his wife.

Next up was another Sicilian dish, a spaghetti pie, constructed like a mountain and stuffed with wood-grilled spiced quail and chunks of salami made from the padrone's prize pigs, which he promised to show us later.

Then came more quail (they abound in the tall grass around here), this time stuffed with savoury pork (same pigs) and apples from the farm.

By now we, who were not used to such stuffing in the middle of the afternoon, were beginning to wilt, but no sooner were our plates whisked away than another course appeared, the pièce de résistance: pork crepinettes (same pigs) with fresh autumn mushrooms picked that morning among the apple trees, served with potatoes browned golden, chopped basil and wild garlic.

Last of all, another mountain, this one of pasticcini, was washed down with bergamotcello before we began the grand tour.

It was difficult enough to get up from my chair, never mind take a five-mile hike around the orchards.

They grow a special kind of apple-pear hybrid, sold in supermarkets the length and breadth of Europe, a highly specialised crop the padrone has personally developed and perfected. Up here no frosts ever came to blight his blossoms and he seemed to have good reason to be cheerful, reaping such a profitable harvest from his idyllic world, so close to heaven that at blossom time it must indeed seem like paradise.

It was a long way round, with much information to absorb, and when we got back there was the yard to inspect, workers to meet, and finally the pigs.

The padrone's prize pigs were kept in gleaming white cement sties with all the comforts of indoor-outdoor living. They were extremely large – five hundred pounders at least – raised, he explained, the traditional way, on a diet of acorns, beets, apples, grains, chestnuts, pumpkin and the choicest dinner-table leftovers. I thought of the Empress of Blandings and how Lord Emsworth would have appreciated this sunny, ruminative scene. As he often reflected, there's something very peaceful about a pig.

In this mellow mood we returned to the terrace, where Tarka regaled us with his repertoire until the sky turned violet, a sickle moon appeared and it was time to go.

As we trundled down the drive I felt certain the Green Vote was in the bag.

18

Vigile

Carolina proved the key to getting the men back to work on the wooden house. She enslaved them with her yellow bikini until the walls seemed to fly into place like a Disney cartoon. For the first and only time I was able to communicate exactly what I wanted.

And this, perversely, was to lead to my downfall.

Just as architetto Napoli's skitch had been abandoned at the boathouse, so a new idea that came into my head one day was able, with Carolina's help, to be added halfway through this project, something any architect will tell you is always fatal.

The idea seemed simple enough: a veranda added to the front of the house, shading it from the burning sun and providing a whole new area for al fresco relaxation, like the deep, shady verandas you see in America. I had visions of a porch-glider, a rocking chair, bamboo tables laden with cooling drinks, kids' toys scattered about, a regular down-home rural idyll.

Tearing up plans and mastering destiny is exciting anyway. Pasquale and co. were quick to agree, and to see the potential for laying it on thick in all sorts of ways.

The first, of course, being cement. The whole front apron would need to be widened.

The devil is in the detail – this is the lesson we who are foolish enough to build houses learn, especially in foreign lands. The digging, drilling, measuring and arguing that went on before the cement lorry could even arrive I won't go into. The knock-on effect of something that had seemed so simple spread like a disease. And halfway through it all Carolina abandoned ship.

Tarka suddenly said they had to leave. The effect on the rest of us was nothing short of catastrophic. I thought Gianni was going to break down completely. Nino and Pasquale were just as devastated, and I myself considered asking her – begging her – to stay. Let Tarka go back to London if he must, this could be her new home. She could take the place of the Greek Queen and rule Galati with her yellow bikini.

But it was just a pipe dream. The big world beckoned, and anyway it would hardly be something one could explain to one's wife. She was simply too beautiful to be passed off as a builder's mate.

Her name lives on in legend and song to this day. You only have to say 'Carolina' to Gianni for him to start swooning, and his wife Enza to start boxing his ears and beating him over the head (this mild form of husband-beating is known, to us anyway, as 'Marouge! or Marouge di Moglie').

There was a lot of arguing about the angle of the slope, which would define the veranda's height and depth, and ultimately the tonnage of cement to be poured. I wanted to continue the slope of the roof without a break, starting at a greater height than Pasquale thought necessary. Without Carolina it was uphill work to get my way, but after only a slight compromise we measured up and started ordering things.

The cement lorry arrived, conspicuous as ever, lumbering up the lane for all the world to see, its drum spinning brightly in the sun, as if to say, 'Behold! The Inglese is at it again!' It was about the most noticeable vehicle on the planet. The thought of those Eyes after all these months – they would not be blind forever.

When it was poured the full glory of the veranda could be visualised, from the great, wide, shiny expanse of new forecourt. Despite my anxieties I could almost see the Romanian abandonment as a blessing. Without it the veranda, nothing short of a total transformation, would never have been.

The wood arrived and the structure was framed: fresh, gleaming wood, a delicious smell of gum in the hot sun, a picket fence along the front on either side of the opening where the steps would lead into the garden. The Emperor Nero himself, on first sight of his golden house, could hardly have felt more uplifted than me.

Then came the bad news. The continuation of the roof slope meant a continuation of roof tiles to cover the veranda. These were not the standard tegoli, but flat floppy things made of some weatherproof material unique to Domenico, by all accounts now closed down by the police.

We looked at each other in dismay. None of us had thought of this fatal flaw.

There was only one thing for it. I would have to call Domenico, whom we'd all roundly abused, and demand, or very possibly beg for, more roof tiles, if he had any. Assuming he wasn't in gaol.

Domenico was as irrepressible as ever. You wouldn't think any of the recent disasters had happened.

'Mister Ian. How are you? Everything is well I hope.'

'No, Domenico, everything is not well. We've run out of roof tiles.'

'I don't think so. You have the full Diana materials in your place – everything I have given that you need.'

'I would hardly say that, Domenico.'

'How you could not have enough roof tiles?'

This was the sticking point. I didn't want to tell him about the veranda. Better he'd sold me short and owed me. I felt entitled to the moral high ground, come what may, after the way he'd behaved.

'I don't know, Domenico. We're short, that's all I know.'

'How much short you are?'

I took a deep breath: 'Ventotto metri quadrati.'

'Ventotto. That's a whole half of the roof! Impossible.'

'Look, Domenico, have you *got* any? I really need them and I think you should help me out, all things considered.'

'I'll look in the warehouse. Maybe there's left over. I'll let you know.'

A couple of days later, rather to my surprise, he called. He had some boxes left, probably enough, only blue. Ours were green.

'No green? You're sure?'

He was sure.

'I'll get back to you.'

I conferred with Pasquale, who immediately had one of his brilliant ideas. We would lay the blue ones on the back slope of the roof, where they couldn't be seen. That should give us enough green for the front slope, including the veranda, where it mattered.

'How soon can you deliver them?' I asked Domenico.

'Deliver them? No, Mister Ian, I am not in business right now. Chiuso – all sealed up. You have to come get them quando non si vede – capisci?'

'But I haven't got a lorry.'

'Camion, no. Carabiniere videre. Bring your car to warehouse mezzogiorno, when carabiniere sleeps.'

'But will they fit in my car?'

'Speriamo.'

And so a few mornings later I set off into the mountains, to Serra San Bruno. I'd emptied out the Clio and folded the back seats down to make a van. The brakes had been squeaking a lot recently, but as I spun up the familiar sunny route, uphill all the way through sun-dappled pines, the heady zestiness of the air braced me against doubt and fear.

This optimism faded slightly as I drove past the vast façade of the carabiniere building. But after a while, hunting for Domenico's warehouse, I found myself among the beautiful ruins of St Brunone's monastery. Built in the eleventh century, much of it still standing despite the ravages of earthquakes, the thought stiffened my sinews. However hazardous my mission, it could hardly be compared to the privations suffered in these hills in days gone by. The monastery still functions, with full Benedictine rigours. We of the worldly persuasion have lost much of our toughness I'm afraid. I took heart from this thought.

I eventually found the warehouse and waited outside as directed. Domenico finally arrived, an hour late, bumptious as ever in his

BMW. With him was a taciturn youth who was sent inside to find the tiles.

'Ciao, Ian,' said Domenico, 'come stai?' He didn't seem any less upbeat and I half-expected him to start selling me some new marvellous thing.

'Bene grazie,' I said. No point being grumpy when he was helping me.

Domenico shook his head in a worldly philosophical way. 'Problemi,' he said.

'Si,' I sincerely agreed, 'sempre problemi.'

Then the taciturn youth appeared, staggering under the weight of a massive flat pack strapped with twine. He toppled it into the back of the car which groaned in protest.

'How many more?' I said, alarmed.

'Cinque.'

When they were all loaded, including one in the passenger seat, the car was so low to the ground it almost covered the wheels. When I got in and started forward it made a horrible grinding noise. It was literally resting on its axles.

I got out again, shaking my head. 'I can't get back down the mountain like this,' I said. I would certainly die in the attempt.

Domenico said, 'Non problema. I show you the flat route to Soverato. Then you drive home on the coast, easy all the way.'

Easy all the way for 160 kilometres it turned out, looking at the map. Not to mention getting there in the first place, which, though not directly down a mountain, was still a descent, shallow for most of the way but not all of it.

I set off gingerly, easing the car forwards.

Domenico called, 'Piano, piano.'

I headed for Chiaravalle as directed, straight and level most of the way. Up hills was bad, labouring fit to burst, and down them was worse. The brakes wouldn't brake unless you prepared them half a mile in advance. I could only pray for nothing sudden to happen.

The road into Chiaravalle was steep, downhill and halfway down it a funeral was crossing. A carabiniere stepped out in front of me and held up his hand.

I pushed my foot to the floor, pulled on the handbrake and prayed. I even think I shut my eyes. There was a dreadful grinding noise and the world stood still until, barely two feet from the knife-edge crease in the policeman's smart blue trousers, we shuddered to a halt.

But the grinding and groaning continued, like an iguanodon in pain. He only needed to turn to see the unroadworthy car, the illegal overloading and the mortal peril he was in.

The funeral was a grand affair with a full brass band, and the sombre tones of Zdenek Fibich's funeral march (if I'm not mistaken) from 'The Bride of Messina' drowned out the hellish groans of the car. The musicians and mourners trailed interminably by, the priest with his incense-swinging altar boys, the huge garlanded hearse, all at the undertaker's solemn pace, until I thought it would never end, except in the death-by-flattening of the carabiniere.

But then at last he turned to smile and wave me on. 'Grazie,' he said, little knowing the narrow escape he'd had.

I ground forward, yelling 'Prego' as loud as I could to cover the awful sounds. I couldn't stop for the cross street but he didn't seem to notice.

The road from Soverato home was by the smiling sea, with few surprises but plenty of traffic lights. I developed a technique of slowing down well in advance, which went down very badly with my fellow motorists.

But I stuck to my guns, so it was a long 160 kilometres. I was desperate to stop for a coffee but something told me it would be tempting fate. As they say in tennis, if you've got a winning game stick to it.

I stuck to it all the way to my turn-off. Dusk had fallen and there was only the starry night to witness my last hurdle, my Becher's Brook, the steep descent under the Bridge of the White Nightingale.

It was a bit like skydiving. I eased myself into position and let go, hugging the left desperately to avoid landing in the river. The car clung to the bank, thumping it violently as I pulled the wheel hard over to use my downward momentum to make it up the steep left-hander into the lane.

Then suddenly we were home. I climbed out and listened to the night. The sea sighed up the beach and a huge cruise ship stole across the horizon, brilliantly lit like Christmas. I could hear the deep rever-beration of its engines carried across the still water. My little car glimmered on the drive – I could have hugged it like a horse – safe and level at last with its precious cargo.

Getting the roof tiles was one thing, but laying them was another. First came a thick layer of insulation, bright blue and highly visible to every train that passed. Then wooden framing had to be sealed with tarpaper, and only then could the tiles be laid, one by one, each overlapping the other by exactly the same amount. It took a long time, the one thing we didn't have.

And unbeknownst to us the sands of time were running out and the hand of fate was poised to deal the deathblow.

It happened one afternoon. As so often with these things, it came literally out of a blue sky. The day was particularly glorious, as early October weather can often be in Calabria, in many ways the nicest time of year there.

But not this time. I was relaxing on the alto terrazzo reading a book, when down the drive came Pasquale, running like seven devils were after him. I'd never seen him run, or panic, before.

'Vigile,' he gasped.

'Vigile?' I'd never heard the word before.

'Telefono Pino. Presto. Subito.'

I hurried to the house and dialled Pino's mobile phone. When he answered I said, 'Pino. Problemi. Vigile.'

But he already knew. 'Si, si,' he said. 'Tranquillo, Ian. Io cognosco. Sto arrivando – I'm coming.'

'He's coming,' I told Pasquale, who was peering nervously round the side of the house at a small white Fiat Panda in the drive by the gate.

When I moved forward to investigate he held me back with his arm. 'No, no – lascia a Nino.'

Nino was talking to someone by the car, who was writing in a notebook. The vigile wasn't wearing a uniform and didn't look at all frightening to me.

But I could tell from Pasquale's manner that this time we were in real trouble. When Pino arrived he confirmed this. The eyes had ceased to be blind.

By then the vigile had left and the story could be told.

Someone had denounced me and the comune had no option but to send the vigile, the lowest form of policeman but nonetheless lethal in cases like this.

The good news, and there was some, was that the vigile had first called Pino to let him know what was happening. Pino, ever active in the system of favours, persuaded the vigile, a distant cousin of some kind, to say the work was finished. Then he alerted Nino and Pasquale to the danger. When the vigile arrived they were ready for him and everyone had their scripts worked out.

The vigile duly inspected the wooden house and wrote in his book that it was finished. This clearly was not the case, but it meant that it could be. If he'd written that it wasn't, all work would have had to cease forthwith.

'What's going to happen to me?' I said, seriously alarmed.

There was a lot of shrugging and shaking of heads.

Pino said, 'Perhaps nothing, perhaps, who knows? Problemi.'

'What kind of problemi?'

'Problemi con tribunale.'

The tribunale in Locri is the place where, apart from being the killing ground of politicians when the 'Ndrangheta wants to make a point, judgement is meted out to offenders like me, of the building or any other code, all of which, in Italy, comes under the heading of 'Criminale'.

I might need a lawyer. If I did Pino would find one. All would be well: 'Tranquillo, Ian – non ti preoccupare.'

In southern Italy everything can be fixed one way or another. Pino would talk to architetto Napoli and see if he'd heard anything.

Meanwhile work could continue and I could sweat it out.

Next day, a Sunday, an engine driver appeared in the drive, complete with large family. This turned out to be the vigile's brother, from whom he'd received such glowing reports of the wooden house that he hadn't been able to resist coming to take a look. He'd often noticed it taking shape from the cab of his train. Being Sunday, he'd brought his entire family for an outing.

The idea that he might be my denouncer flashed across my mind, but on reflection it seemed unlikely. He was so friendly and jolly it seemed impossible he could be a Judas. Anyone on any train could have seen those glaring blue insulation tiles. And then there was the professore – the very embodiment of a dagger-wielding Iago.

After they'd examined the wooden house from top to bottom they started on the rest of the place. No stone was left unturned. When they got to the garage they unearthed a stash of musical instruments, including a drum kit.

'Strumenti! Bellissima strumenti!' exclaimed his two teenage sons, one of them banging experimentally on a snare drum.

I admitted that my own sons were musicians.

'My boys too!' said the engine driver. Next year, when my family returned, perhaps they could all get together and make La Musica.

Over the next few days several other friends and relations of the vigile came to admire the wooden house, all very fulsome in their praise, wishing they could have one too. His aesthetic attitude clearly differed sharply from his official one.

Towards the end of the month architetto Napoli reported back to Pino what might hopefully be achieved with the comune.

'He will prepare the papers for a condono at the next amnistia.'

'What does that mean?'

Pino explained the profitable system Mr Berlusconi had worked out to regularise illegal building.

'You must pay.'

'How much?'

'One hundred euros per metri quadrati.'

At fifty-four square metres, that would be 5,400 euros, plus 'a bit more for the comune.'

The logic of the system, if you can call it that, is that the amount is what it might cost you to prepare an application for permission beforehand, were it not for the fact that there is no permission.

'And the tribunale?'

Pino shrugged, 'Maybe some problems, maybe not. We have an avvocato who works there.'

'A fine?'

He shrugged again.

'They won't make me knock it down?' This was my deepest fear.

Pino looked astonished. 'Why would they do that?'

'In England if you build an illegal building they make you knock it down.'

'In Italy all building is illegal.'

19

How to Buy a Pig

The pig is as central to Calabrese life as the grape and the olive, and anyone who can buys one and rears it in his garden, Gianni included.

Gianni's family home is large, with a big, cool, underground garage, all built by Gianni.

There are no cars in the garage. It's been given over completely to wine and salami-making. Barrels and bottles line the walls, and from the roof beams hang a plethora of sausages and hams. A grape press and an ancient sausage grinder with a crank handle complete the picture.

The word 'salami' embraces a wide variety of sausage-type meats, dolce and picante and otherwise: soppressata, capocollo and the spreadable 'nduja, but also Calabrian pancetta (more like bacon) and the Calabrian sausage, which doesn't take so long to mature, and which can be packed with all kinds of ingredients, according to the whim of the manufacturer.

Gianni was keen to introduce me to the noble art of sausage- and salami-making, according to Gianni. He'd just slaughtered one pig and was about to buy another. I'd be able to learn the process from the ground up, so to speak. At least I'd missed the killing part. The beast was hanging by its hind legs among the previously made salamis, looking very big and pale.

The intestines had been removed to make the skins and Gianni brandished the large intestine at me, laughing hysterically. He'd expected me to recoil in horror and I did.

He said, 'For 'nduja.'

The name meant nothing to me, but after what followed I am now something of an authority.

First he ground some raw meat in the grinder, explaining in his usual patient way that it was 'secondo' – lesser cuts like shoulder, thigh and underbelly. He then passed it all through a big sieve and he finally ground a lot of his beloved super-hot peperoncino into it. Our eyes were streaming by this point.

When he was happy with the result we took some of the meat through to Enza to cook for lunch.

When it was ready the whole family sat solemnly down for the taste test. Once it got the thumbs-up Gianni and I returned to the garage where he stuffed the large intestine with the mixture until it was tightly packed, tied it off and hung it from a beam.

'Un anno,' he said. It would be a year before becoming Gianni's version of the spreadable salami 'nduja, one Calabrian thing at least that has caught on worldwide.

There was still some mixture left, and this he stuffed into a long tube of small intestine. He twirled it expertly into the kind of sausage string you see in old-fashioned butchers, what he called a 'catenella', and hung it up.

'Una mese solo.' These sausages could be cooked and eaten in a month. He would bring me some.

Then came the main event: soppressata Calabrese. I was ready to go home by now, but Gianni insisted, in his usual stubborn way.

For soppressata the meat comes from the thigh or shoulder. Gianni sliced some of both off the pig and proceeded to mince it with a lethal-looking knife so it was very coarsely chopped. Then he sliced off a great, white, translucent layer of thick subcutaneous fat from under the skin of the pig's back, diced it into small chunks and mixed it in by hand with powdered peperoncino, pig's blood, red wine, sea salt, oregano, garlic and mashed-up sweet red peppers until the whole mixture turned bright red. Then he squeezed it expertly into six-inch-long tubes of intestine, tied them off with gut, and piled them up ready for smoking in his garden smoke-shed.

It all sounds simple enough, but the hidden ingredient is the indefinable essence of 'locale': the fact that Gianni has been doing it all his life, and his father and forefathers before him. It's in the soil and the mountain air, the pigs' feed, the salt smell off the sea, and the peculiarly Gianni one in his garage, his kitchen, his garden. Then there's what T. E. Lawrence called 'the irrational tenth, like the kingfisher flashing across the pool' that makes it uniquely Calabrese, or Palizzese, as Burgundy wine is to the golden slopes of Burgundy. You can try it at home, but it won't taste the same.

I gained further experience the following week when Gianni appeared in the drive and announced that he was off to buy a new pig. Would I like to come?

When I said yes he asked if we could go in my car. Enza was using his.

This was very unusual, but I thought nothing of it and off we went. We were to meet up with Pasquale and a cousin of his, who was also a cousin of the pig farmer, on the back road into Bova Marina.

Sure enough there they were, waiting for us in a clapped-out-looking Fiat Panda 4×4.

We all got out and went through the greeting process, introducing me to the cousin, whom I'd actually met before. He lived in Palizzi Superiore and was fanatical about football. I've been to Palizzi Superiore and seen the trophies in their only bar. It isn't hard to imagine, in so remote a place, how on long winter evenings a person might become fanatical about almost anything.

Seeing me again was like the red flag to the bull. The fact that I was English automatically meant, as far as he was concerned, that I must be an equally fanatical supporter of Chelsea or Manchester United, or some other sworn enemy of Juventus.

The QPR get-out didn't work with this guy – he knew all about QPR – nor was it any good saying I wasn't interested in football. That would have brought to the surface the latent hostility that simmered just beneath his macho, joshing, shoulder-punching manner.

'Hey, Inglese,' he said, gripping me round the shoulder in a vice-like grip that was just too close for comfort.

'Hey, Paolo,' I said, as heartily as I could.

'Chelsea.' He knew I lived in Chelsea and no amount of explaining in my limited lingua was ever going to change his mind about which club I support.

'Juventus!' I echoed, and luckily he left it at that.

He led the way, driving as aggressively as he did everything, turning without warning off the road up a narrow blind hairpin I'd never noticed before.

It was a rough stony track – not really a road at all – that went up a steep hill in a series of blind bends made blinder by being behind Paolo, whose Panda kicked up dust and stones into my windscreen like a desert storm.

On the rare occasions we could see anything the view was spectacular. We were high up what amounted to a cliff-face, looking out across hundreds of miles of sea.

Then we headed inland at breakneck speed. Pandas are good at this, high off the ground and built to last, probably the least appreciated all-terrain vehicle in the world.

Not so the Clio. Mine was strictly a road car, and one whose recent experience as an HGV had left it in need of a complete overhaul.

I clung on as best I could, dropping back a bit on the assumption that the road probably ended in a pig farm and that Gianni must know the way anyway. It was the competitive thing with Paolo that had kept me on his tail like a demented Stirling Moss.

Sure enough the track led to a metal gate that opened onto a wide concrete yard. There was a house on the left with a large dog sleeping on the step. All the rest were pigs.

The layout was simple: row upon row of open cement sties with gullies for water and waste set into the cement floor. The thing went on for miles, and every sty was crowded with pigs, pink as babies, grunting, oinking, squealing, jostling, snuffling, shoving each other, mounting each other, their small piggy eyes glinting as they looked up when we passed. There were far too many pigs per sty, nothing like the luxurious conditions enjoyed by the fruit-farmer's prize porkers.

Gianni and co. joined the pig-man in expertly selecting a suitable animal. This involved what seemed to me a lot of needlessly cruel poking and kicking and generally insensitive behaviour. But then I reflected that this was the way it had always been since the days of the Emperor Augustus. Nothing has changed, even the cement. They have cars and mobile phones, but just beneath the surface these men are of the same ancient race that has inhabited these shores since the most distant antiquity, children not only of the Empire but of aeons long before that, a cruel and brutish world of survival just as rough as here and now in Calabria, uniquely preserved in an otherwise totally altered world.

I couldn't have it both ways. Politically correct behaviour towards pigs is all very well, but it goes hand in hand with other PC things far less welcome. I suddenly had the strangest sensation of having travelled back into the Ancient World. Just for a fleeting microsecond, but all the same, it was the thing I'd been seeking, and now at last I'd found it, here in this pig-poking place, where ancient and modern meet. If a legion had marched up the hill behind us it would, in that flickering moment, have seemed perfectly normal.

When Gianni finally made his selection, the pig, a big pink porker with a bristly attitude, got a sharp whack on the rump from the pig man to separate it from its mates. It left its sty and scampered off at high speed, hotly pursued by Gianni and Paolo.

Pasquale took me aside, ostensibly to show me something. We walked the length of the pig farm and looked up at the mountain beyond. Nothing seemed to be happening there – the few sheep grazing on a grassy slope were hardly noteworthy.

'Bella vista,' said Pasquale, gesturing at the great beyond.

This was very unlike him. Pasquale is no idle admirer of landscapes, especially this one, which he sees every day. Something was up, but I couldn't for the life of me imagine what.

I soon found out when we got back to the forecourt. There was

something very wrong about my car. I didn't get it for a moment –
the sense of déjà vu was too strong. It was down on its axles again, if
anything more so, just like on the great roof-tile run.

Then when it started rocking I saw the pig. He was looking at
me through the back window. They'd folded the seats down and
somehow crammed the enormous animal in the back. Now they
were lying on the ground laughing, tears streaming down their
faces, howling at the afternoon sky. I turned to Pasquale, but he'd
wandered over to a bench and sat there, shaking and heaving with
mirth.

They'd planned the whole thing, ever since my overloaded car had
given them the idea.

For as long as they could, they clung to the idea that I was going
to drive the pig home, and I went along with it – it was a better joke
that way. But the pig was finding it less and less funny, and getting
more and more restless in the tight confines of the Clio.

He had to be let out eventually, and when they lifted the hatch-
back he sprang to the ground with extraordinary agility. They had a
lot of trouble catching him again, but it had been worth it. He was
loaded into the pig-man's Piaggio three-wheel wagon, and I kept the
windows of the Clio open all the way home.

That night Gianni insisted on taking me out for a pizza. Maybe
he thought he'd gone a bit too far with the pig – I couldn't tell. Or
maybe it was to celebrate his prize purchase. Either way I couldn't
really refuse, though a break from speaking Italian would have been
very welcome.

We were going to a place he knew on the way to Reggio, but first
Enza wanted to visit a new furniture store she wanted me to see. It
closed at eight, so we left around six.

We'd hardly left Spropoli before Gianni made his first stop. Enza
needed to visit her father, something she always did when passing.
Gianni and I waited in the car. The minutes ticked by.

We got going again eventually, but just past Condofuri Gianni
suddenly turned off the road up a track.

'Momento,' he said, and disappeared into a ramshackle shed, leaving the engine running and the door open.

I asked Enza what on earth was going on. She shrugged, 'Non lo so. Motore di barca possibile.' There were a lot of engine parts lying around, so this seemed feasible.

We waited and waited. Twenty minutes later he appeared in the doorway with a man in overalls who was wiping his hands on an oily rag. I thought we were off, but they stood there talking like they had all the time in the world.

Enza didn't seem anything like as restless as a wife should be, and I reflected for the umpteenth time on the extraordinary timekeeping of the Calabrese. They don't seem to have the slightest sense of urgency. Time passes, but not for them. They treat it as static, and maybe this is how they've managed to remain totally unchanged in an ever-changing world. They've deliberately got left behind, like someone at a bus stop letting bus after bus go by, in their case the one to Progress and the Modern World.

Eventually Gianni got in and got on with it, with no explanations from him or remonstrations from Enza. We drove along as if nothing had happened.

We were approaching the outskirts of Reggio when the next stop occurred. Gianni suddenly jerked to a halt outside a small bar and exclaimed, 'Caffè.'

This he explained was the bar of a friend of his, where he always stopped on his way to and from work, the implication being that he couldn't pass it without stopping. Politeness and habit and the possibility of free coffee dictated this.

We trooped in. By now I was past caring. It wasn't my deadline. I was just being English thinking life was a race against time. I set myself resolutely to enjoy my coffee and the free apricot brioche that came with it and the very long incomprehensible conversation with Gianni's friend.

When we arrived in Reggio Gianni and Enza did at last get into an argument, about where the store was and how to reach it. She thought he knew and he thought she did. When we finally got there it had been closed for half an hour. Gianni said 'M'a.'

'M'a' summed it up nicely. In Calabria when anything goes wrong it's always 'M'a'.

The mood was philosophical as we headed back the way we'd just come. These things happen. There was always tomorrow.

The pizza place was on the main road and impossible to park near. When we did find a space it was a long walk back, followed by a life-threatening crossing.

The outside looked cosy, with a neon pizza sign and straw umbrellas. But once through the door it expanded into something far vaster, emptier and more barn-like even than Pino's most gigantic eateries. Two disconsolate waiters leaned on their elbows behind a bar. There wasn't another customer in sight, yet one of them took us miles, to a lonely spot near the largest television I'd ever seen.

Gianni seemed delighted. 'Bellissima,' he said, beaming round the trackless waste of empty tables. Size does seem to be the yardstick of excellence when the Calabrese eat out.

He opened an enormous menu and said, 'Pizza.'

After a very long time indeed our waiter returned and we ordered our pizza. Gianni told the pig story over and over again, partly for Enza, partly for the sheer joy of reliving it. In the background the TV commentator became increasingly excited about a football match, the roar of the crowd blending like a laugh-track with the pig story.

At the end of the meal and the final re-telling Gianni raised his Coca-Cola glass to mine and toasted, 'Amici.'

I said, 'Grandi amici.'

Enza said, 'Simple friends.'

'No, no,' I said, 'friends are friends.'

There's really nothing simple about it.

20

The Immense Fence

At our farewell festa Bunty had become quite pally with the professore and he'd gallantly promised he'd build her a fence. I didn't like the idea, preferring to keep my destiny in my own hands. He was about the last person to decide its position and, in particular, its height.

Bunty maintained that having built the offending storey he ought to pay for the fence (which he agreed), and therefore ought to be allowed to build it. Let him have all the bother and expense.

But this logic was upside down. The only thing that mattered was to make his giant eyesore go away and this wasn't going to happen without something spectacular. It needed to be fifty feet high.

November came with no sign of any fence and I decided to act. I'd be going home soon for Christmas and the fence had to be up before I left, with all its planting complete.

I convened a conferencia with Gianni, Pasquale and Nino. We gazed up at the giant edifice and Gianni said gloomily, 'Troppo alto.'

I gestured in the most Italian way I could and said, 'Rete – rete grande, rete MOLTO grande.'

If we could only find the right uprights we could stretch fencing wire between them and grow things up it. A simple fence, but on a vast scale. This was the picture I was attempting to paint. It will be 'semplice', I said.

Even Pasquale shook his head, but then Nino, taciturn as ever, nodded his and said, 'Si, semplice.'

Nino had a cousin who worked for whatever department it was

that ran telephone wires up and down mountains to remote sub-scribers. This in many cases involved extremely tall telephone poles. He would see what could be liberated.

Next day he arrived with them on his flatbed, sticking out front and rear, seven of the tallest telegraph poles I've ever seen. We laid them on the grass and looked at them in awe and wonder. They really did look a match for the prof's massive edifice, but how to secure them?

Again Nino stepped into the breach. His pneumatic drill was on board and the yellow cement mixer had never left the premises (it still hasn't).

Once the plan of action was worked out we set to, me included. The existing boundary fence included a low wall, and this was breached in seven places, allowing deep cement footings to be sunk. We finished the one in the centre first, tied ropes to the first pole, then, on the word 'Adesso!' we heaved. Nino, bent like a Scottish caber-tosser, lifted the base of the pole into the still wet cement. Then more cement was poured until it reached the surface. The ropes were tied to secure it and we all stood back. It soared skywards like Cleopatra's Needle. For the first time I felt a surge of real hope that this grandiose project might actually work.

The professore wasn't there that day, and by evening all seven poles were in place. I thought it important to present him with a fait-accompli, so the following morning we started early. Nino arrived with bales of strong wire netting piled high. The cement had set, and the tricky part began.

Now the great adaptability of the Calabrese came into play. I've never known there to be anything they can't do once they've set their minds to it. I suppose that part and parcel of the totally non-urban life they lead is that all of nature is their hymn sheet.

In this instance they all but turned into monkeys, swarming up the poles, clambering along the wire once it was in place, moving from section to section, tightening, securing.

I stood and watched, moving restlessly from spot to spot to gauge the height. There was no doubt about it: the poles were level with the professore's roofline. If the planting was as successful, the privacy of the Villa La Buntessa might yet be saved.

The final section overlooked the professore's own front garden, tucked behind his sea wall. Unlike mine, his wall is high and enclosing, as is his whole perimeter. He likes his privacy to the point of paranoia.

The fence gave whoever happened to be clinging to it, in this case Gianni, a grandstand view, just as the professore emerged from the house. He'd arrived without us knowing, while we were otherwise engaged.

There now followed a very significant sequence of events. Gianni, happy in his crow's nest, called out amicably, 'Ciao, professore.'

Gianni, a local, has known the professore, who comes from Reggio, for at least twenty years. Though the professore is a professore, and Gianni a bus driver, Italy is a republic in which all are truly equal, not just theoretically, like in America. However high he might stand in his university, here the professore is a visitor in Gianni's world, and by the code of manners which strictly applies in southern Italy, owes it to Gianni to be at least polite.

This code the professore now proceeded to breach. He turned his back on Gianni and, refusing to answer, stalked back into his house.

Gianni was mortally offended. He still talks about it to this day. At the time it served to fuel the anti-professore feeling needed to side with the foreigner against him, something I never took for granted. The work proceeded with renewed energy.

A deep trench needed to be dug along the base and a watering tube laid. Once this was done we were ready to plant my hedge.

Most hedges around here are oleander, pink and white. They are the obvious choice, quick-growing and colourful. The plants start at eight to ten feet tall and grow taller quickly.

And they're easy to find. But I'd become fatally attracted to a hibiscus hedge I'd seen, exotic, multi-coloured and beautiful. I knew it could be done because it was growing beside the road near Brancaleone. I took Pasquale to see it.

There are nineteen varieties of hibiscus suitable as hedge plants available locally and all of them come from Franco.

I'd made a vow to avoid Franco and his Byzantine billing system at all costs, but now his sheer virtuosity, his profound knowledge of plants and trees, his genuine enthusiasm for me and my 'Eden' became irresistible. He was the only game in town, and what's more he could deliver, advise, plant and generally enter into the spirit of the thing.

For him it wasn't just Christmas, it was Easter and New Year as well. His truck came trundling down the drive as of old, absolutely laden.

What he hadn't mentioned was the addition of a row of fourteen acacia trees at 100 euros a pop. But when I saw them and learned that they flower and grow to fifty feet in a year or two, I had to agree they were a definite plus; a second line of defence.

Meanwhile the nineteen varieties – all the colours of the rainbow and more, singles, doubles, triples even – went in along the base of the immense fence, interspersed with 'rampicante' varieties of jasmine, plumbago and white wisteria, which would hopefully climb and riot all over the upper reaches of the fence in clouds of blue and white, filling the air with exquisite aromas and utterly obliterating what lay beyond.

It was a very hopeful and a very expensive experience. Franco took over, and as November drew to a close, presented his bill: 190 hibiscus plants @ 20 euros = 3,800 euros. 14 acacia trees @ 100 = 1,400 euros, plus other sundry items, the climbers, planting, plant food, transport, labour, you name it, brought the grand total to a round 7,000 euros.

But seven is a lucky number, and as I viewed the immense fence with its green baseline sprouting up, already partially obscured by the advance guard of rustling acacias (there's something very satisfying about planting trees) I was filled with renewed optimism. The devil in my garden had been held at bay. The bottom of the barrel had been scraped. It was time to go home.

Before I left, Pino came to inspect. It was a sunny day and he'd brought his swimming trunks. He admired the fence and challenged me to a November swim. I decided to brave it. It would be good to go home and say I'd swum in November.

The water was clear as glass and cold as ice, and the deeper we went the clearer it got – you could see the bottom for miles. We stayed in until our blood matched the water and tingled through our veins, a tonic that renewed my faith in the magical powers of the Ionian Sea.

When Pino left he said there was one more thing. As president of the Bova Marina Choral Society he wished to formally invite me to their pre-Christmas concert, in the Oratorio Salesiano of the Church of the Madonna dell'Isodia, an event of which he was both organiser and star. It was to be 'a very formal affair', and he begged me to at least try to dress accordingly.

I'd fallen sadly short of Pino's hopes and expectations in this respect. As a grande scrittore Inglese he had imagined, when first we met, that my dress sense would match the prestige of my position.

But it doesn't. I don't have a suit, and only one tie, a Craigie Aitchison that wouldn't have done at all – a pink and yellow parrot painted on vivid green silk.

It was a bit hot for sweaters, but I wore one under my double-breasted jacket, a Paul Smith copy that I bought years ago for a brief and fruitless attempt at wedding-driving in my mother's Bentley Continental, and which now serves all formal purposes.

The trousers were the real let-down, a choice between the chequered chef's in which I'd arrived and a pair of rumpled jeans that wouldn't do up any more after all the pasta I'd eaten.

I laid books along the jeans for a couple of days, in hopes of a crease. They were at least quite dark, and in the dimness of the church (I imagined) might go unnoticed. The unfastened waist-stud was hidden under the all-encompassing sweater.

The place was packed when I arrived – all to the good. I crept in unseen and made my way to a dark pew near the back. It was extremely hot. I looked around covertly for Pino's family. It was essential they should know I was there, yet not get to see me close up.

Sure enough, there was Celeste beckoning me to join them in the front row. I was in the middle of a series of hand gestures to indicate something, I didn't know what exactly, to excuse myself, when there was a mighty blast on the organ and the curtain went up.

The massed choristers of Bova Marina were arranged in a wedge shape in front of the altar, the prow of the wedge being Pino in a tuxedo, jutting out into the audience like the figurehead of a ship. To say he was the star of the show would be a serious understatement.

He led all the singing in a powerful bass baritone, his bow tie and white shirt-front, coupled with his large frame and prominent position, dominating the proceedings. The Byzantine-Romanesque rafters reverberated to his voice for several hours, during which time I got hotter and hotter.

Afterwards we foregathered in the small piazza of the church. There was no way to avoid this. Slinking off into the night, which I so desperately wanted to do, was out of the question.

Yet when the moment came that I'd been dreading, of the invitation to dinner at one of Pino's barn-like restaurants, I surprised myself.

Perhaps unconsciously moved by forces latent in the house of God, I came up with something inspired. Taking account of the language barrier, and with my jeans still relatively invisible among the massed trousers around me, I said that after all that beautiful music I couldn't imagine anything I could bear to listen to now other than the Music of the Sea.

Musica del Mare. It was the first time I'd ever turned down an invitation, and on this night of nights to boot, but it struck exactly the right chord. You could see it in their faces. The scrittore Inglese had hit the poetic nail on the head.

Feeling extremely fraudulent I climbed into the Clio and drove away, their sympathetic voices ringing in my ears: 'Musica del Mare.'

And there it was. After the mighty rushing wind, the still small voice. Along the coast road, in the silent night, the dark pines silhouetted against the starry sky, the moon laying its long silver path across the water: the music of the sea.

I got out of the car beside the house and listened to it. Soon I would be back in London for Christmas. It was hard to imagine. There'd be carols round the crib and Christmas pud, but there'd be tabloid headlines too, and the relentless onslaught of populist propaganda that makes our overcrowded island such a ticking bomb of bad tempers. After a year in Calabria the culture shock was going to be severe.

But in spite of all temptations to belong to other nations, I remain an Englishman. If I wasn't I couldn't be an Englishman abroad.

Post Script

Seven years have passed and still nothing much has changed in the Altro Mondo. But the writing is on the wall. Just on the other side of our local village of Galati a 'villaggio' is being built called the Jewel of the Sea, which threatens to change everything. There will be swimming pools and shops, tennis courts and a beach club, a five-star hotel and even a golf course. And there'll be English voices in the bars and cafés for the first time (apart from mine). I won't be the only Inglese in town any more.

Just as it was for the Roman Empire, so the first crack has appeared in the fabric down here that must inevitably lead to Decline and Fall. The Barbarians are at the gates.

To begin with it looked bad, but opinion was fiercely divided. There would be jobs and foreign money. The non cambios didn't agree. Look what happened in Spain. For a long time everyone had an opinion and the topic was on every lip. Then all of a sudden all work ceased and the Jewel of the Sea looked liked joining the ranks of unfinished buildings that line the coast hereabouts like unsightly brick-and-mortar ghosts.

The whisper went out: 'Ndrangheta. Perhaps they didn't like the Jewel of the Sea, or they'd fallen out with them, or something. Who could say? For a while it looked hopeful that we could carry on in our time warp forever after all, the one place on Earth that never changed.

Then that September work resumed. Men were seen moving among the skeletal uprights, laying bricks and turning gaps into walls. Hearts sank or rose, according to their point of view. Nobody knew anything, but that didn't stop them having plenty to say.

Then in October it stopped again and the place was deserted once more. Who can tell what the future holds?

Pino never got to be mayor of Bova Marina. Darker forces, so the rumour goes, prevailed. Now he concentrates on his dentistry and surgery, and seems all the happier and richer for it. His popularity and importance in Bova are undiminished, but he no longer needs to exploit it. He's bought a big plot of land in a gated community just outside the town and built a palazzo suitable to his prestige, like one of those rare Roman emperors who were able to retire without being murdered.

Gianni taught me how to plant my own ort when I returned in the spring. We rotivated the soil in front of the wooden house and down one side of the orchard, then laid rows of watering tubes. We bought the tiny plants in Bova Marina: pomodoro (three varieties), pepperoni, melanzane, peperoncino, zucchini and basil: hundreds of plants for just twenty euros.

Gianni made holes with a pointed piece of wood he called a 'pipi-tuni' (his own word), and we dropped in the plants, fertilised them, watered them and watched them.

It was like a miracle – you could almost see them growing. The soil here is wonderfully rich and fertile. On a clear day Mount Etna's white peak can be seen shimmering through the haze, and when it erupts the volcanic ash descends on the soil, fertilising it with life forces torn from the bowels of the earth. In a few weeks we were cutting cane to make frames for the tomatoes.

By late June things were ready, a riot of green, with fat red tomatoes, golden zucchini flowers and glowing purple aubergines, the whole area fragrant with basilica.

This was good for business, because we'd rented the place, and picking your own vegetables was one of the attractions.

The money had more than run out and to keep things going we'd advertised in *The Lady*.

The ad for our 'undiscovered paradise' was very cheap and the response amazing. English families were eager to brave these unknown regions. Neither the mafia nor the complicated journey was going to deter them. I was surprised, delighted, and more than a little apprehensive. The wooden house still wasn't finished and the barakka is an acquired taste at the best of times. Bunty and I were both extremely nervous about whether we were going to end up on the wrong end of lawsuits from a lot of irate holidaymakers.

For the first group – the pioneers so to speak, or guinea pigs – I retreated to the San Giorgio to monitor events. I'd put Pasquale in charge, and Nino's wife Maria was drafted in to be the 'maid'. They don't have a word of English between them, but both were keen to give the intrepid Inglesi the holiday of a lifetime.

The idea was that the arriving party would call Pasquale on his mobile phone once they'd landed at Reggio and were en route to the house via the detailed directions given. This would give him half an hour to get there, open the gates and prepare himself to welcome them. I told them he didn't speak English, but when he heard an English voice on his phone he'd know.

I stayed out of it, waiting in the San Giorgio with bated breath. The signora and her family were equally riveted as the hours ticked by. No news must be good news was what I hoped. Speriamo! But I went to bed unconvinced.

Next morning I'd still heard nothing so I decided to drive over and see what was happening. I honestly couldn't believe it had gone without a hitch. Perhaps they hadn't arrived.

But they had arrived, and were very much in evidence as soon as I got through the gates. Two teenage boys were playing ping pong and two teenage girls badminton. Mum and Dad were sitting on the veranda having a nice cup of tea.

'Care to join us?' they said. It was a most peculiar feeling, being a guest in your own home, drinking out of your own cup while another's mother poured.

'No problems?' I said, rather tentatively.

'Absolutely not!' said the dad. 'This place is fantastic. That fellow Pasquale is an absolute star!'

And so it turned out. Pasquale took to his role as the grande controllare like a duck to water. Year on year since then the renters have arrived and left without a hitch, all their problems solved by Pasquale. When the electricity suddenly goes out, or the lav gets blocked, or a rat appears in the barakka, or the well breaks down (which it does with monotonous regularity) or they need to know where to find the best pizza, Pasquale is there for them, his English as non-existent as ever, but his ability to communicate second to none. I don't know what he gets out of it – maybe some of them cross his palm with silver. But on the whole I think he just loves meeting them all, and being their Calabrese Admirable Crichton.

The wooden house saga dragged on for five more years, what with lack of funds and the legal Sword of Damocles hanging over it. Wooden walls alone do not a habitation make, was one thing I learned. Even when finally up it still needed tiling on the floors, a bathroom, wiring, lighting, plumbing, painting, ad infinitum.

Then one morning in London I received a terrifying document through the mail, covered in official Italian seals and full of words like 'criminale'. It was from the tribunale in Locri. I rang Pino in a panic.

'What shall I do?'

'Tranquillo, Ian. Post it to me. All will be well.'

The lawyer he found lived in Spropoli, a young woman with a piercing voice who lived with her parents. The alarm she inspired in me was offset by the parents, who, once she'd left on her furiously busy way, always sat me down in their garden for a chat and a glass of iced espresso, which her mother kept in the freezer, and for which she is justly famous. The peace in the garden would gradually calm my fears of prison or deportation or worse. I can safely say I never understood a single word she said to me. I can only understand Italian spoken slowly, or by Gianni or Pino or Pasquale. She spoke fast and loud, and with a terrifying impatience that thoroughly unnerved me.

In the end it all came down to a small fine, or a small fee, I never understood which. I handed over the money (480 euros) in the kitchen and we, Pino included, toasted the occasion with iced espresso. The daughter was laughing and smiling, so I assumed (wrongly it now seems) I was off the hook.

This event triggered the condono, handled by architetto Napoli, which was much more expensive, but at last made the wooden house legal. The documents are pinned to the wooden wall, now painted white on the inside, and multi-coloured on the outside, by Bunty.

She had the idea of using Cuprinol, which comes in lots of lovely colours and costs very little. I took a load down there in our Toyota people carrier which we bought cheap from a man in south London, and which now serves as a means of transport for the ongoing programme of improvements that never seems to end. In April I load up, mostly at Ikea, plus clever finds of Bunty's, and drive for four days through France and Italy. It doesn't make sense in one way, but it does in another, like so many things.

On the wider stage of life, soon after this, we received some shocking news. Tarka had committed suicide. He hung himself from his bedroom door with a belt, Michael Hutchence-style. He was the last person I would ever have thought of doing that. He was much too vain and amusing, and anyway I wouldn't have thought he would know how – the thing with the belt sounded much too complicated.

No one could understand it. There didn't seem to be any warning or sense. One minute he was there, next we were all mourning at Mortlake Crematorium. I've never seen so many pretty girls gathered together in one place. We went to his brother Barney's local in Fulham afterwards and everyone had a theory. Mine is that maybe Reality got to him, in a sudden dark moment, a rip in the fabric of fantasy, and his flair gave out. Living like he did is a bit like walking on water. Maybe, like Saint James, he made the big mistake of looking down.

Whatever the reason, he's gone and the part he played in my life is important to me. He helped me in a dark moment when I wasn't sure whether what I'd done was tantamount to jumping off a cliff. He renewed my wavering faith and reminded me of what had inspired me in the first place. He loved Calabria and the Villa La Buntessa, his father Denny's name for Bunty, and every year I scatter bougainvillea petals on the warm Ionian water in his memory.

The immense fence is an immense success, a screen of green which every year grows denser and more like a vast plant in its own right. This is due in part to the professore himself, whose own vines rushed rapidly over the wire and gradually strengthened the structure with their stems. My plants took longer, but now the jasmine has reached the top and so has the wisteria. The hibiscus hedge is taking its time, but it has dawned on me that the one near Brancaleone has probably been there for fifty years. I need to take the Capability Brown view (piano, piano). Every so often, in moments of despondency, it puts out a flower of such transcendent beauty that all is forgiven. One day it will be a tall hedge of glorious flowers. The question is, will I still be around to see it?

Epilogue

It's almost two years on from the sentenze and the wooden house is still standing. But the Sword of Damocles hangs over it. The blow might fall at any time. Or on the other hand it might not.

Last year Pasquale greeted me at the airport with a triumphant smile.

'Casa di legno ancora.'

'Pasquale. Tutto bene?'

'Per adesso si. Non smontare.'

'E comme tu resolveresti questo?'

Pasquale stuck his fist in the air and said, 'Resist!' The word is the same in both languages apparently.

He had found an 'avvocato con più d'esperienza' in dealing with the tribunale. She said that no appeal was possible after all these years. Her advice was as follows:

'Do nothing and say nothing.'

What happens to people who ignore sentenzes of the tribunale, and whether another sentenze might follow involving 'manacolo' and the penitenziaria I didn't like to ask. Meanwhile all is well from day to day, which is how life is lived around here. Doing nothing and saying nothing likewise.

The Jewel of the Sea villaggio in Galati never materialised in the end. That is to say it did, but then it finally stopped for good, leaving it part built and abandoned. Rumours abound, the most popular being that the whole thing was a criminal enterprise from the start involving IRA bank-robbery money combined with funds from both the Naples Camorra and the Calabrese 'Ndrangheta. The Jewel of the Sea is now not only a wasteland but a crime scene. Many arrests have been made. The Irish boss is reportedly on the run somewhere in Africa.

Things have sunk back to normal once more and life has resumed its timeless pace of going nowhere in our small forgotten paradise of nothing. There will be no flocks of tourists spending money in the shops and bars of Brancaleone and Galati, no much-needed work for hundreds of people, no increase in prosperity on the Jasmine Coast. Just the usual flocks of sheep.

And the popular reaction to this? Relief. Not just by me but by people in general. Despite habitual hardships people are happy with things the way they are. In some unspoken and instinctive way they know that all progress is bad, and that they're much better off as they are, left alone and ignored by the wider world – abbandonato. The sun continues to shine on three hundred and twenty-six days of the year, the fish continue to teem, the goats to graze on the mountainsides, the fruit and vines and vegetables to grow prodigiously in the warm volcanic soil. Life is good.

My family and I keep going back as the years go by and I'm sure I always will as long as I can, to the place that never changes. In the end it will all end and we will all end. In the meantime, as someone said, all that remains is Love.

Acknowledgements

First and foremost I want to thank my wife Bunty, for putting up with my whims and obsessions over the years, most recently in Calabria, and for loving me and going on loving me. From the moment I first saw her she was all I ever really wanted in this world.

To my brother-in-law and old friend Charles Glass for reading the book and liking it enough to show it to the publisher who liked it enough to publish it.

To Piers Russell-Cobb who is that publisher, who took a chance on an author who hadn't published anything for too long.

To all my friends and neighbours in the magical time-warp world of Palizzi (RC) who you are about to meet.

To my many children and grandchildren, all of whom are an inspiration in one way or another, and without whom getting older would be much more boring than it is.

To Carly Robertson for doing all the stuff I can't do – there's nothing she can't do!

And finally to my brilliant editor Eleo Carson, without whose wisdom and friendship I could not have done it; as Stephen King once said, 'To write is human, to edit is divine.'